Thomson Round Hall

Employment Law

Dorothy Donovan

DUBLIN
THOMSON ROUND HALL
2006

Published in 2006 by
Thomson Round Hall Ltd
43 Fitzwilliam Place
Dublin 2
Ireland

Typeset by
Siobhán Mulholland

Printed by
ColourBooks, Dublin

ISBN 1-85800-454-3

A catalogue record for this book
is available from the British Library.

Table of Contents

Table of Legislation

STATUTORY INSTRUMENTS

EUROPEAN MATERIAL

INTERNATIONAL AGREEMENTS

TABLE OF CASES

1. INTRODUCTION

This introductory chapter gives a simplified overview of employment law in Ireland. Each of the main topics will be dealt with in more detail throughout the book. Extensive use has been made of *Irish Employment Legislation* (Anthony Kerr, ed., Thomson Round Hall, Dublin), which is an excellent source for further information and reference.

There are four main sources of employment law in Ireland: the common law which is the earliest source, the law of equity which can provide a remedy where damages are inadequate or inappropriate, the Constitution and statute law. It is the law of contract, and to a lesser degree tort law, that plays a role in the employment area. Sources under the Constitution are in the nature of rights. But it is statute law, which is increasingly driven by the European Union, that is now a major source of employment law.

The introduction of the Employment Equality Act 1998, The Equal Status Act 2000 and The Equality Act 2004 means that there is now a degree of overlap between employment and equality law.

OUTLINE OF IRISH EMPLOYMENT LAW

Irish employment law, whatever the source, is concerned with rights, duties and obligations of employers and employees. In general terms, employment law is concerned with the relationship between employer and employee and the incidents of the employment contract, such as the conditions and terms under which employees are hired and fired, where and when they will work and the manner in which they are treated during the term of the contract of employment. Irish employment law may have an application prior to employment and in situations where a person does not in fact become an employee at all; there are now legal requirements that have implications for the recruitment process in areas such as advertising, the selection process for interview, how the interviews are conducted and the selection of persons for employment.

APPLICATION OF EMPLOYMENT LAW

The rules and principles of employment law apply only where there is a relationship of employer and employee. There will be many situations where, on the face of it, there appears to be such a relationship but where in fact there is not. The essential feature in deciding whether the relationship of employer and employee exists is the existence of a contract *of* services rather than a contract *for* services (discussed later in this book at Chapter 2). Moreover, certain persons although called *employees* are in fact officers or office-holders. Although all of the features of a contract of services may exist they, nonetheless, fall outside the legislation, for example, civil servants, members of the Defence Forces and of An Garda Síochána. Some trainees/apprentices and employees who work less than a certain number of hours per week may also find themselves outside the scope of many of the employment law statutes. Additionally, most of the statutes have a qualifying service period before employees may avail of the benefit of them.

EMPLOYER AND EMPLOYEE RIGHTS, DUTIES AND OBLIGATIONS

At the core of employment law is the concept of rights, duties and obligations. Although employment law grants rights to and imposes duties on both employer and employee, it mostly tends to create liability for employers while granting rights to and protecting employees.

These rights, duties and obligations may arise either from contract (the contract of employment between the parties) or from the legislation (the statutes). In general terms, both employer and employee are under an obligation to observe the terms of the contract of employment and the provisions of the legislation.

Duties and Obligations of the Employer

The employer has a duty to comply with the terms of the employment contract and with the relevant statutory provisions. The employer, *inter alia,* must furnish the employee with the essential terms of his/ her employment contract in writing within two months of the date of employment. The employer is subject to an extensive duty of care. Such duty includes an obligation to provide both a safe system of work and safe place of work which should include, *inter alia*, a bullying and harassment policy. The employer may also be required to indemnify the employee in respect of any liability that may arise from the contract of employment and to treat the employee with fidelity.

Duties and Obligations of the Employee

Although employment legislation is now largely rights-based in favour of the employee, the employee, nonetheless, has duties towards his employer. Again, these duties and obligations may be contractual or statutory, and include: a duty to perform the employment contract with competence and care, to follow instructions and to obey reasonable orders of the employer, to be cooperative, to indemnify the employer from liability where appropriate and necessary, not to do anything to bring the employer or his business into disrepute, not to abuse any of the rights due to him/her either under the contract or under the legislation and to act with fidelity towards his employer.

THE COMMON LAW

The common law impacts on employment mainly in the area of contract law and tort law. Of the two, contract law is the more significant.

Contract Law

Rules and principles of contract law apply in the employment context because all employment relationships are based on contract between the parties. All of the well-developed rules and principles of contract law apply to the employment contract. Thus, there must be offer, acceptance, consideration and agreement to create legal relations. The contract will be subject to equitable principles and rules and is also subject to modification by the provisions contained in the various employment law statutes. The contract will generally be written, but there is no requirement either under the law of contract or under the legislation that it be reduced to writing. All that is required under the legislation is that the employee be supplied with written confirmation of the terms of his/her employment within two months of the commencement of employment. The employment contract may, in addition to the express terms, contain implied terms, in particular those implied by statute law. Once it is established that there is a valid contract, all of the remedies available under the law of contract become available to the employer and employee when there is a breach of all or any of the terms (see Chapter 2).

Tort Law

There are a variety of duties imposed on persons over and above whatever obligations are imposed under contract. In the employment context, the duty of care that employers owe as regards their employees' safety while at work is the most important. In this regard, the courts have laid down a variety of obligations in tort. These duties have been supplemented and expanded by statutory provisions such as The Safety, Health and Welfare at Work Act 2005 and provisions prohibiting harassment in the Employment Equality Act 1998 (see Chapter 4). Liability in tort may arise for personal injury and tangible damage to property and, exceptionally, there can be tort liability for purely financial loss.

EQUITY

Equity plays a role in the employment context by providing the equitable remedies of injunction and specific performance in situations where damages (compensation) is not an adequate or appropriate remedy. In the case of senior executives/employees and public office holders, equity may impose fiduciary duties owed by these persons to their employers over and above those duties that arise by virtue of the contract of employment.

THE CONSTITUTION

The Constitution impacts on employment law as follows:

First, there is a requirement that the legislation does not contravene a provision of the Constitution. If it does and an affected person, employer or employee, brings a constitutional challenge, the piece of legislation in question may be declared invalid.

Secondly, since 1965, the courts have held that there is an unspecified personal right to work and earn a livelihood in Art.40.3.1 of the Constitution.

Thirdly, the equality guarantee contained in Art.40.1 of the Constitution has the ability to guarantee non-discriminatory treatment between the sexes and others in the workplace. However, the implementation of the various pieces of equality legislation, in particular the Employment Equality Act 1998, has somewhat diminished the need to use this constitutional provision where there is a claim of discrimination.

Fourthly, where there has been a breach of fair procedures in any employment action, a claim may be made in appropriate cases that constitutional justice has not been afforded, particularly where an affected person is an office-holder rather than an employee.

THE LEGISLATION

Legislative provisions are contained in the Acts of the Oireachtas, Statutory Instruments or Regulations. Much of the legislation since 1973 has been driven by Ireland's membership of the EEC/EU and thus, many of the enactments are underpinned by Directives of the EEC or the EU. The following are the main statutes which are currently in force (see Chapter 3):

- Industrial Relations Acts 1946–2001
- Protection of Young Persons (Employment) Act 1996
- Minimum Notice and Terms of Employment Acts 1973–2001
- Unfair Dismissals Acts 1977–2001
- Payment of Wages Act 1991
- Maternity Protection Act 1994 and Maternity Protection (Amendment) Act 2004
- Terms of Employment (Information) Act 1994
- Adoptive Leave Acts 1995 and 2005
- Organisation of Working Time Act 1997
- Parental Leave Act 1998 and the Parental Leave (Amendment) Act 2005
- Employment Equality Act 1998
- National Minimum Wage Act 2000
- Carers' Leave Act 2001
- Protection of Employees (Part-Time Work) Act 2001
- Protection of Employees (Fixed-Term Work) Act 2003
- Protection of Employees on Transfer of Undertakings Regulations 2003
- Employees (Provision of Information and Consultation) Act 2006

THE FORA

If a claimant wishes to pursue an action under the employment legislative code, the forum will be the statutory tribunals, one of the tribunals set up under the legislation. These statutory tribunals are:

- The Labour Relations Commission (LRC)
- The Employment Appeals Tribunal (EAT)
- The Labour Court
- The Office of Director of Equality Investigations (ODEI)

Many of the statutory actions have a right of appeal to the Circuit Court and all have a right of appeal to the High Court on a point of law.

The particular statute under which the action is being taken will decide in which tribunal proceedings are to be instituted and will indicate where there is a choice of fora open to a claimant.

A claimant may litigate an action in the civil courts, usually the Circuit Court or High Court. Where a claimant expects to secure damages of less than €38,000, the Circuit Court will be the appropriate forum but where the claimant hopes for a higher sum, he/she should go to the High Court. Injunctive relief may be sought in the court where the substantive (main) action is being taken. An action for recovery of wages, where the amount is small, may be litigated in the District Court as a debt against the employer.

A claimant cannot, however, pursue the same action through the courts and the legislative tribunals. An election must be made whether to proceed via the courts or via the statutory tribunals. Thus, if a claimant elects to take his/her action in one of the statutory tribunals, the jurisdiction of the courts is ousted as against that action, unless the particular statute under which the action is taken allows for a right of appeal to the Circuit Court and/or thereafter on a point of law to the High Court. However, in appropriate cases, the claimant who has pursued his/her action through one of the statutory tribunals and who feels that the procedures by which the decision of the statutory tribunal was reached was procedurally incorrect or who feels that the decision was irrational, may still be able to access the courts by way of judicial review.

In addition to the venues listed above, many employees may have available to them in-house mediatory/arbitral processes. Before litigating a personal injury claim it must firstly be referred to the Personal Injuries Assessment Board (PIAB).

DEFENCES TO A CLAIM

Not every claim by an aggrieved employee will necessarily succeed. What may appear, prima facie, to be a valid complaint by an employee may be capable of defence by the employer. The nature of an employer's defence will depend on the type and circumstances of the individual claim. The possible defences open to an employer could, *inter alia*, include:

- The forum in which the employee has instituted proceedings lacked jurisdiction.
- In the case of a claim of unfair dismissal or wrongful dismissal, the employer might be successful in demonstrating that there was justification either because of the claimant's conduct or the claimant's lack of competence or qualifications.
- The dismissal was not, in fact, a dismissal but was a bona fide redundancy carried out in accordance with law.
- Continuing to employ the claimant would put the employer in contravention of a statute or in breach of the law.

REDRESS/REMEDIES

The remedy at common law will usually be damages and, in equity, the equitable remedies of specific performance and injunction may be available in appropriate cases. Relief, by way of judicial review, may also be available. Statutory relief consists of re-instatement, re-engagement and/or compensation. The remedies and redress available at common law, in equity and under statute, in practice, are not dissimilar. For example, the relief of damages available in the civil courts is similar to compensation available statutorily and injunctive relief and specific performance can achieve the same purpose as re-instatement and re-engagement. The equitable remedies of injunction and specific performance, like all equitable remedies, are discretionary, so too are the statutory remedies in that the statutory tribunals can award whatever redress, if any, the tribunal considers appropriate, having regard to all the circumstances (see Chapter 8).

2. THE EMPLOYMENT RELATIONSHIP

The main items for consideration in this chapter are the contract of employment, who qualifies as an employee, who is an employer and what are the rights and duties of each towards the other. (For a more detailed discussion see, for example, *Employment Law* (Michael Forde, 2nd ed., Round Hall Sweet & Maxwell)).

THE CONTRACT OF EMPLOYMENT

As mentioned in the introduction, all employment relationships are based on contract between the parties, not least because a person is only defined as an employee in law where his/her relationship with an employer is based on a contract of services. It is important to distinguish between contract *of* service and contract *for* services. If there is a contract of services, there is an employee but if there is a contract for services there is an independent contractor rather than an employee. See *Henry Denny & Sons (Ireland) Ltd v Minister for Social Welfare* ([1998] 1 I.R. 34). The employment legislative code applies in the main to employees only. Thus, if a person is an independent contractor, he/she may not have statutory rights or protection under the various employment law statutes. See, for example, *In the Matter of an Appeal pursuant to Section 271 of the Social Welfare (Consolidation) Act 1993 and In the Matter of Castleisland Cattle Breeding Society Limited v Minister for Social and Family Affairs* ([2004] 1 I.R. 150). Further, an independent contractor may qualify as an employee for the purpose of health and safety legislation. There is no requirement that the actual contract of employment be in writing. See, for example, *Mairead Carey v Independent Newspapers (Ireland) Ltd* ([2004] I.R. 52) where the plaintiff successfully sued for breach of contract on an orally negotiated contract.

The contract of employment may be in the nature of a collective agreement.

In all spheres, freedom to contract on whatever terms the parties so wish is restricted but none more so than in the employment sphere, where freedom of contract is severely restricted by legislation and such legislation leans heavily in favour of the employee. Importantly, a provision in any contract that seeks or purports to exclude or limit the application of many of the Acts is void.

Whereas a contract may be oral, the Minimum Notice and Terms of Employment Act 1973 and the Terms of Employment (Information)

Act 1994 place an obligation on employers to supply a written statement of the essential terms of employment to employees within two months of their commencing the employment. The Minimum Notice and Terms of Employment Act also provides for a minimum period of notice prior to termination of the employment relationship and the Organisation of Working Time Act 1997 lays down requirements as regards maximum working time and the organisation of working time of the employee as regards annual leave, public holidays and daily and weekly rest breaks.

Employee contracts that do not contain a clause relating to gender issues, either expressly or by reference to a collective agreement or otherwise, will have one inserted into it by s.21 of the Employment Equality Act 1998, while s.30 inserts into every contract of employment, which does not already contain one, a non-discriminatory equality clause.

Even the privity of contract rule is affected by employment legislation; see European Communities (Protection of Employees on Transfer of Undertakings) Regulations 2003 (S.I. No.131 of 2003) whereby a contract of employment entered into with a previous employer will be transferred to the new employer on a transfer of undertakings, *i.e.* the new employer is now a party to the contract which was entered into between the previous employer and the employee. Also, under these Regulations the common law position that the contract of employment automatically terminates on the sale of a business is no longer in effect and on a transfer of undertakings all the transferor's rights, powers, duties and responsibilities under, or otherwise arising, in connection with a contract of employment are transferred, subject to an exclusion concerning employees' pension entitlements.

Whereas the parties may agree as to what wages or salary are to be paid, the rate agreed must not be less than the rate set under the National Minimum Wage Act 2000. The methods used for the payment of wages and salaries and the deductions that may be made from wages and salaries is regulated by The Payment of Wages Act 1991, irrespective of what the contract provides.

In fact, almost every piece of employment legislation may affect the contractual terms. The contract may even be varied as time goes on by the introduction of new legislation and it will generally be to no avail for an employer to say that a particular piece of legislation was not enacted at the time of the contract.

Once it is established that there is a valid contract, a breach of it will attract all of the contractual remedies available at common law under the law of contract, both for the employer and employee alike. Alternatively, redress may be available under the legislation. It should be noted that as far as most contractual rights and obligations are concerned, it is of no regard whether the person engaged to perform work for another is an employee or otherwise. However, where the person is an employee, certain terms will be implied into a contract of employment that will not be implied into other types of contract and it is of crucial importance as regards redress under the legislation whether a person is an employee or self-employed.

EXPRESS TERMS OF THE CONTRACT OF EMPLOYMENT

The express terms included in a contract of employment will include, *inter alia*, the job title/job description, place of work, the date of commencement, in the case of a fixed-term contract—the length of the fixed term, whether there is a probationary period, working times, holidays, whether shift work is involved and if so the time scales, the salary or wages, rates of pay, frequency of pay, deductions from pay, bonus or commission payments, details of expenses, details of "perks" such as cars or other benefits in kind, notification requirements regarding absences due to illness or otherwise, whether sick pay will be paid, pension entitlements, normal retirement age, notice period on resignation or termination, a confidentiality clause and/or a restraint of trade clause if appropriate, details regarding disciplinary or grievance procedures and details regarding possible changes in the terms of employment. If the contract of employment is in respect of an executive employee, it may contain additional terms such as appointment and duration, duties of the appointed executive employee, who the appointee is to report to, whether the appointee may be seconded to another associated company, details regarding conflict of interest and post termination obligations of the appointee.

TERMS IMPLIED BY LAW OR IMPLIED/MODIFIED BY STATUTE

The employment contract may, in addition to the terms expressed in it, contain terms implied under the law of contract by the operation of certain common law doctrines, implied by custom and practice in the particular industry or implied by judicial intervention. Most frequently, however, the employment contract will contain terms implied by legislation. The following illustrates instances where terms may be implied.

Notice

Where no notice period is expressed in the contract of employment the courts will imply a reasonable notice period. In *Royal Trust Company of Canada (Ireland) Ltd and Another v Kelly and Others* (unreported, High Court, February 27, 1989), it was stated that the basic rule in relation to contracts of employment is that "it is an implied term of every contract of employment other than one for a fixed period that it can be terminated upon reasonable notice". What is reasonable notice will depend on the facts of each case such as, *inter alia*, the position the employee in question holds in the company and the length of service. See, for example, *Carvill v Irish Industrial Bank* ([1968] I.R. 325), where reasonable notice for an employee holding the position of managing director was held to be one year. Irrespective of what notice period is specified in the contract of employment, s.4 of the Minimum Terms of Notice Act 1973 provides that the minimum period of notice must be given by an employer who wishes to dispense with the services of an employee or by an employee who wishes to leave his/her employment (see further Chapter 3).

Example: Thomas has been employed by Grace Sisters Limited as a Managing Director. He is supplied with a written contract which does not contain a "notice" term. He consults his solicitor who advises him that whereas it would be prudent that the position regarding notice be clarified, that notwithstanding, Thomas has dual protection regarding notice even in the absence of an express term in the contract of employment in that the courts will imply a reasonable notice period into the contract. Additionally, the Minimum Notice and Terms of Employment Act 1973 provides for minimum notice periods and a method for calculation of same depending on length of service at the time of termination.

Holidays and Working Times

Although an employer and employee are free to contract as regards holiday entitlements, any such arrangement agreed between the parties must comply with ss.19 and 20 of the Organisation of Working Time Act 1997. Section 19 provides for a new four-week holiday entitlement (see further Chapter 3).

Salary and Wages

The Payment of Wages Act 1991 dictates the modes by which wages or salary are to be paid and what deductions from wages or salary are permissible, irrespective of what is contracted between the parties.

Example: Grace Sisters Limited deducted, without consent, an amount from all their employees' wages in respect of a store raffle. When questioned about it, the wages clerk told the employees that in their contracts of employment there was a clause that deductions for items such as PAYE and PRSI may be made from wages. The wages clerk pointed out that the words "such as" meant that the list of deductible items was not exhaustive. The employees are concerned and take advice from their union representative who ascertains that the deduction in respect of a raffle does not fall into a category of items such as PAYE and PRSI and that in the absence of an express contractual term, the deduction for the raffle is unlawful and in contravention of the Payment of Wages Act 1991.

Provisions in any contract of employment or other agreement to pay less than the national minimum hourly rate of pay are void by virtue of the National Minimum Wage Act 2000 (see further Chapter 3).

Sick Pay

Whereas there is no automatic entitlement to sick pay, there is authority for the proposition that wages or salary should be paid even in the event of illness, unless the parties have agreed otherwise. Thus, in the absence of a term covering what is to happen if an employee is absent due to illness, a term will be implied that the employee is entitled to sick pay. See *Rooney v Kilkenny* ([2001] E.L.R.) and *Charlton v Aga Khan's Stud* ([1999] E.L.R. 136) where an injunction was granted compelling the employer to pay sick pay in the absence of an express sick pay provision in the contract.

Termination/Dismissal

Unless a contract is stated to be for a specific or fixed term, the contract
is deemed to be for an indefinite period and whereas the contract can
provide that termination or dismissal may occur on the happening of
certain events, nonetheless, such termination or dismissal must be in
accordance with the provisions of the Unfair Dismissals Acts 1977–
1993 (see further Chapter 7).

Discrimination/Equality

Section 21 of the Employment Equality Act 1998 provides for the
insertion of a gender equality clause into an employee's contract, which
does not already contain one. Thus, an employer cannot offer more
favourable terms to one employee over another employee based solely
on the fact that one is a woman and one is a man (in the Act referred
to as the "gender" ground). This Act also contains an equal pay for
equal work provision as between men and women. The net effect of
this is that an aggrieved employee can sue for breach of contract.

Example: Grace Sisters Limited employed Mary and Thomas in their
computer department. Mary is very well qualified, having successfully studied for a degree in computer science. Both Mary and Thomas
have the same job title and perform the same duties. A promotion is
advertised in the department. Both Mary and Thomas apply. Thomas
is the successful applicant. When Mary queries this with the HR department, she is told it is company policy to promote male employees
over female employees. Because there is a gender equality clause implied in her contract of employment, Mary may, as an alternative to
pursuing a discriminatory action under the legislation, sue for breach
of contract.

Restraint of Trade

A restraint of trade clause in a contract of employment must be
considered in the light of the law of contract, the Constitution and
competition law, *viz.* the Competition Act 1991. Whereas the parties
are free to include a term prohibiting the freedom of an employee to
carry on an activity which adversely affects a former employer, such
clause or term will be unenforceable if it is too broad—and it may also

be in breach of s.4(1) of the Competition Act 1991. Notwithstanding, an employer is entitled to protect the commercial know-how, trade marks and business secrets, both during the employment and following cessation of employment. See *Facienda Chickens v Fowler* ([1986] 1 A.E.R. 617), where a former sales manager left his employer and set up a rival distribution business and solicited clients of the former employer, using customer lists which he himself had developed during his time with the company. Of critical significance was the total absence of any term in his contract relating to the use of information or restrictions on competition. The former employer sought an injunction to prevent the use of the lists and the soliciting of the clients. The Court of Appeal listed three classes or types of information that might be applicable to such a case:

(1) Trivial Information or information already in the public domain. This information was never confidential and its use could not be restrained.

(2) Confidential Information which is information not generally available to the public and which comes to the employee's knowledge in the course of his/her work. The court said that the use and dissemination of such information could be restricted but only by means of a written contract and that restriction must be reasonable in its terms.

(3) Trade Secrets. Their use and dissemination can be restrained even in the absence of a written term. Effectively, there is no temporal or geographical restriction on the right of the employer to these.

On the facts of the instant case, it was held that the information was confidential information but in the absence of an express clause its use could not be restrained in the present circumstances.

Similar in nature to restraint of trade clauses are anti-compete restrictions. The position here is that it is possible to restrict the post-termination or post-cessation competition but only by use of an express term. Clearly, competition whilst the employee still works for the employer can be restrained even in the absence of a clause and can also be the basis of a dismissal. See, for example, *Greg Coleman v Ove Arup & Partners Ireland* (UD 816/2002). A post-termination anti-compete clause must meet the test of reasonableness (see *Warner Bros v Nelson* ([1957] 1 K.B. 209—the *Bette Davis* case) and *Page One*

Records v Britain ([1962] 1 M.L.R. 157—the *Troggs* case). At common law, it must be reasonable in terms of time and space (see *Nordenfelt v Maxim Nordenfelt* ([1894] A.C. 535) and the more modern case of *Esso Petroleum Co Ltd v Harpur's Garage Ltd* ([1968] A.C. 269)). Ideally, the temporal aspect should not be greater than three months otherwise an employer may run the risk of it being deemed unreasonable and geographically, it should not be greater than the employer's market place. For example, if the employer's market is Dublin only, there should be a Dublin district restriction only. Best practice dictates the least amount of time and space as possible. See *Murgatroyd & Co. Ltd v Purdy* ([2005] 3 I.R. 12) where "a twelve month prohibition period and a geographical restriction based upon the jurisdiction of the Irish State were not unreasonable".

Good Faith

The law of contract will imply into contracts of employment as against both parties—employer and employee—a duty to act in good faith (see *Mallick v BCCI Bank* ([1997] 3 A.E.R. 1)). In *Reilly v Minister for Industry & Commerce* ([1997] E.L.R. 48), this duty was referred to as the duty to act fairly.

THE PARTIES TO THE CONTRACT OF EMPLOYMENT

The parties to the contract of employment are the employer and the employee. The question as to who is an employee seems unproblematic—in theory—but in practice it has and continues to present some difficulties.

Who is an employee?

There are two main legal categories of persons who work for others. They may be employees or they may be self-employed. Most employment legislation defines who is an employee for the purpose of the particular Act but nevertheless, it may still fall to the courts to decide whether a particular person is an employee or not. The courts have used various approaches or tests such as the integration test, the enterprise test and the control test in determining who is an employee. The authorities, both Irish and English, are inconclusive in so far as it is not possible to point to a single authority that gives cast iron guidance on the issue. However, the principles in the case of *Henry Denny & Sons (Ireland) Ltd v Minister for Social Welfare* ([1998] 1 I.R. 34) appear to be the accepted principles *vis-à-vis* who is an employee for the purposes of the legislation. These principles are:

- That notwithstanding the requirement to examine the terms of the written contract in determining whether a contract was of or for service, regard must be had to what the real arrangement on a day-to-day basis between the parties was. A statement in a contract to the effect that a person is an independent contractor is not a contractual obligation but merely a statement which might or might not be reflective of what the legal relationship between the parties was.

- That in deciding whether a person is employed under a contract of service or under a contract for services, each case must be considered in light of its own particular facts. In general, a person could be regarded as providing his services under a contract of service and not as an independent contractor where he was performing those services for another person and not for himself.

- That the degree of control exercised over how the work was to be performed, although a factor to be taken into account, was not decisive. An inference that a person was engaged in business on his own account could be drawn where he provided premises, equipment or some other form of investment, where he employed others to assist in the business or where the profit derived from the business was dependent on the efficiency with which it was conducted by him.

See also, *In the matter of an appeal pursuant to Section 271 of the Social Welfare (Consolidation) Act 1993 and In the matter of Castleisland Cattle Breeding Society Limited v Minister for Social and Family Affairs* ([2004] 1 I.R. 150).

The problem with the *Henry Denny* principles is that they are only applicable to the type of employee in that case, *i.e.* demonstrators or similar type workers who were not permanent full-time employees. It can be distinguished from every other case. There is no clear situation where you can be absolutely guaranteed that it will stand up. The case may stand alone.

A good way of approaching the issue is to:

- Examine carefully the features of the work relationship.
- Examine very carefully the contract.
- Engage in a balancing exercise with reference to the appropriate individual authorities such as *Graham v Minister for Industry and Commerce* ([1933] I.R. 156); *In Re Sunday Tribune* ([1984] I.R. 505); *O'Coindealbhain v Mooney* ([1990] I.R. 422); *Tierney v an Post* ([1999] E.L.R. 293) and *Henry Denny*.
- It would be a mistake to consider any authority to be the last word on the issue.

Features of the work relationship/contract of employment to be considered include:

- How is the remuneration paid? Is it gross, without deductions therefrom? If so, it points towards a contract for service and therefore self-employed, independent contractor rather than an employee.
- What is the situation regarding VAT? Where the worker is charging VAT on top of fees then there is a strong indication of independent contractor status rather than employee.
- Where remuneration is paid on foot of invoices, particularly where VAT is charged, there is a very strong indication of independent contractor status.
- How does the worker present himself for the purposes of income tax to the Revenue Commissioners? This is not conclusive but it certainly gives an indication as to whether the worker thinks of himself/herself as an employee or self-employed.

See *DPP v Martin McLoughlin* ([1996] E.L.R. 493) and *Minister for Social Welfare v Griffiths* ([1992] I.R. 103), where the EAT held "that a designation of one kind or another by the Department of Social Welfare cannot be a deciding factor though the manner in which tax and PRSI is paid is a factor which is looked at by the Tribunal".

The Control Test

This test examines control and supervision. The control test asks whether the employer can control not only what is done but how it is to be done. Clearly, the higher the degree of control, the more likely the finding of employee status. This test requires consideration as to whether the worker can generate a profit from his endeavours and/or whether he/she risks a loss. The Supreme Court considered this issue in *Tierney v An Post* ([1996] E.L.R. 293) which concerned a post master who sought to establish that he was an employee of An Post. In support of his argument, he pointed to the considerable degree of control that An Post had over his work. The Supreme Court held that he was not an employee but was an independent contractor. The relevant factors in support of this holding were the fact that he was required to provide his own premises, he was entitled to hire his own staff and he took on risk or losses, as well as profit.

In *Martin McMahon v Securicor Omega Express Ireland Limited* ([2002] 13 E.L.R. 317), the EAT in deciding that the claimant was an employee were "influenced by the significant degree of control that the respondent had had over the claimant." The claimant had had little opportunity to operate on his own and had had no opportunity to profit from his venture. He had worked a full day at a rate set by the respondent. The claimant had carried little risk in relation to profits and had not insured the goods he carried. In *Frank Doherty v Kincasslagh Trawlers* ([1999] E.L.R. 251), the claimant worked as a fisherman on the respondent's boat and was paid by share. Remuneration was always based on catch and if no fish were caught during the period at sea, then the crew would not be paid. The claimant submitted that he was an employed person and that he contributed only his labour and that the respondent had exercised control over him. The respondent submitted that the relationship between the parties was in the nature of a partnership. The EAT held "that the element of control was a factor which was consistent both with the existence of a contract of service and a partnership agreement".

The Integration Test

The integration test or approach asks whether the worker is "part of the employer's business". See *Re Sunday Tribune Ltd* ([1984] I.R. 505). In *Readymix Concrete* ([1968] 2 Q.B. 407), the issue was whether or not the plaintiff's employees qualified for state pensions. If they were employees, they would qualify, but not if they were independent contractors. The employees' work was examined.

- The workers were owner drivers. They purchased their concrete trucks from the employers by way of a hire purchase agreement. The truck was owned by the individual worker himself.
- The trucks in question were painted the company colours.
- The drivers wore company uniforms.
- The workers were obliged to carry out the employer's orders.
- They were paid on a mileage basis.
- The contracts described the workers as independent contractors.

The court examined all the foregoing features. First, it was held that the description of the parties in the contract is not of itself conclusive but of significance was the fact that the workers owned the instruments used to carry out the business. This fact rendered them effectively individual business persons, albeit small business persons rather than employees. This was so, notwithstanding that the company exercised a considerable amount of control over them. However, the control test was not used here.

Approach taken by the EAT to Contracts of Employment

The EAT has a tendency to try to find in favour of employee status. Its decisions are difficult to predict unless your case is close to the facts of a previous decision. See *Duijne v Irish Chamber Orchestra* ([2002] E.L.R. 255), where a cellist was found to be an employee notwithstanding that he owned his own instrument, he was paid gross remuneration and he was free to take on other engagements when he wasn't playing with the Irish Chamber Orchestra. However, there was a degree of control exercised over his playing as part of an orchestra.

In *Kane v McCann* ([1995] E.L.R. 175), the ability to delegate to another person was the deciding factor in finding that there was an independent contractor rather than an employee. In *Ryan v Shamrock Marine Shannon* ([1992] E.L.R. 19), the claimant was found to be an independent contractor. The factors that swayed the decision were the non-deduction from remuneration, freedom to take on other work and the ability to engage third parties to fulfil the duties.

In *McAuliffe v Minister for Social Welfare* ([1995] I.L.R.M. 189), a case which involved delivery men for a wholesale distributor of newspapers, the facts of relevance were as follows: there were two delivery men; both of them worked between five to seven days per week; both were paid monthly on foot of invoices submitted; they owned their own vehicles and covered all the outgoings such as insurance, motor tax and petrol; they were entitled to employ a substitute driver with company approval who they paid themselves. The company wasn't obliged to give them work. They were free to carry goods for other persons but if they were carrying newspapers for the company, they were prohibited from carrying newspapers for any other company. Both of the individuals made self-employed tax returns and one of them was registered for VAT. They were responsible for any delays. The social welfare officer found they were employees. They appealed to the High Court where Barr J. found that the contract was more akin to a haulage contract and he held they were independent contractors.

The Incidents of the Employment Relationship

The incidents of the employment relationship, in essence, means the rights and obligations that each party, the employer and the employee, has in regard to the other. These rights and duties will arise from two distinct sources, one being from the contract of employment itself and the other arising under legislation.

The main duties and obligations of an employee include a duty to perform the employment contract with competence and care, that is to perform his/her work duties—to follow instructions and to obey reasonable orders of his/her employer, to be cooperative, to indemnify the employer in certain appropriate circumstances, not to do anything to bring the employer or his business into disrepute, not to abuse any of the rights due to him/her either under the contract or under the legislation, and to act with fidelity towards his employer.

Thus, the employee is obliged to attend at his/her place of work during the times agreed and to perform the work supplied, provided that the tasks to be performed fall within the ambit of the job definition or job description and are in accordance with any relevant legislative provisions. There is no obligation on the employer to furnish actual work to be done. Provided the employer pays the agreed remuneration for the work period, the employer fulfils his obligation in this regard (see *Turner v Sawdon & Co.* [1901] 2 K.B. 653). However, if it is agreed between the parties that the work is to be paid for on a "piece work" or commission basis then there is an obligation on an employer to furnish sufficient work to enable the employee to earn such remuneration as would reasonably be anticipated (see *R v Welch* (1853) 2 E. & B.357). Employers have a comparable duty of fidelity to their employees. The employer is under a duty to abide by the obligations placed on him/her by the various employment statutes, in addition to those obligations expressed in the contract of employment or implied into it. Importantly, implied into the contract is an extensive duty of care which the employer is subjected to (see *Matthews v Kuwait Bechtel Corporation* ([1959] 2 Q.B. 57)). This duty of care, though founded in tort, now has statutory gloss by virtue of such legislation as the Safety, Health and Welfare at Work Act 2005.

The Duty to Obey Reasonable Orders

The duty to obey reasonable orders is a duty that falls on the employee only. Employers are entitled to expect obedience to orders that are reasonable and not manifestly unreasonable and that are to be performed within normal working hours. Orders that must be obeyed must firstly be reasonable. See *Ottoman Bank v Chakarin* ([1930] A.C. 277), where the court held that a refusal by a bank employee to obey an order to transfer to a branch in Turkey—because of fears for his safety—was not unreasonable. Rather, the court considered it was unreasonable to order the employee in the circumstances to so transfer. Secondly, the orders that must be obeyed must be confined to orders to be carried out during normal working hours. Lawful and reasonable orders and instruction must not only be obeyed but must be obeyed in a reasonable manner and not in such a way as to disrupt the system, the efficient running of which he/she is employed to ensure (see *Secretary of State for Employment v A.S.L.E.F. (No.2)* ([1972] 2 Q.B. 455)). Employers are not generally entitled to give orders as to what employees do outside their working hours. However, there are employments that warrant the giving of certain instructions as to what employees should or should not do while not actually at work. Such orders should not unduly interfere with a person's human or constitutional right not to have their private life interfered with.

The Duty to Co-operate

The duty to cooperate falls on both the employer and the employee. In general, it requires that both the employer and the employee perform their various obligations, contractual or statutory bona fide. As to what constitutes lack of cooperation, see *Secretary of State for Employment v A.S.L.E.F. (No.2)*, which concerned a "work to rule" by train drivers and which was held to be in breach of the employee train drivers' contracts; it breached an implied term to perform the contract in such a way as not to undermine its commercial objective. To discharge their duty to co-operate employers must, *inter alia*, disclose information that would significantly bear on decisions employees may take (see, for example, *Scally v Southern Area Health Board* ([1992] 1 A.C. 294)).

The Duty of Fidelity

The duty of fidelity devolves on employer and employee alike. The extent of the duty is unsure but generally the duty does not extend so far as to make employees fiduciaries for their employers. In exceptional circumstances, the duty may so extend where, for example, the employee is an executive director of their employer's company or where the employee holds a special position of trust, as with a senior public official.

3. THE LEGISLATION

This chapter contains a summary of the main statutes with a more detailed account of statutes dealing with terms of employment, remuneration, working time, employees other than permanent full-time employees, employers' insolvency and what happens when a business or undertaking changes ownership. The chapter also contains a list of how statutes define the various terms.

The following are the main employment law enactments in chronological order with a brief summary of each.

Minimum Notice and Terms of Employment Act 1973

This Act prescribes minimum periods of notice which must be given to an employee in the event of a dismissal. The Act also regulates the notice period. Importantly, the First Schedule to this Act shows how service is to be computed.

Unfair Dismissals Act 1977–2001

This Act, as amended, is one of the most significant pieces of employment law legislation. The first Act was introduced in 1977. Collectively, the Acts provide for statutory intervention and/or redress arising out of an actual or constructive unfair dismissal of an employee. Redress may consist of re-instatement, re-engagement and/or compensation.

Protection of Employees (Employers' Insolvency) Act 1984

This Act confers on employees, in the event of the insolvency of an employer, certain rights such as the right to claim payment of debts arising from the employment relationship, which have not been paid because of the employer's insolvency, from a fund set up by the State known as the "Insolvency Fund". The Act also imposes an obligation on the State to protect the interests of workers in relation to pension schemes. Additionally, the Act amends certain enactments relating to the rights of employees, such as standardising the number of normal working hours required by an employee to qualify for rights under employment rights legislation.

Protection of Young Persons (Employment) Act 1996

This Act replaced previous legislation dating from 1977. The Act regulates the employment and working conditions of children and young persons and raised the minimum age at which a child may work to 16 years of age, with limited work allowance for children of 14 and 15 years of age, mainly during school holidays. It is largely criminal legislation in that it provides for criminal penalties against contravening employers. There is a limited civil remedy and in some circumstances compensation may be paid to affected young employees.

Redundancy Payments Acts 1987–2003

This legislation regulates dismissals due to redundancy. The Act confers a right to fair procedures as regards selection for redundancy, a right to notification and information and time off to seek new employment. There is also an entitlement to a statutory lump sum in the event of redundancy.

Payment of Wages Act 1991

This Act regulates the payment of wages and deductions from wages. This Act also allows an employee to litigate a relevant dispute cheaply and quickly.

Terms of Employment (Information) Act 1994

This Act repeals and updates previous legislation such as the Minimum Notice and Terms of Employment Act 1973 relating to the provision by employers to employees of the essential terms of their employment.

Maternity Protection Act 1994 and the Maternity Protection (Amendment) Act 2004

These Acts provide for maternity leave and related matters such as the right to return to work after such leave, the right to equal pay and conditions and regard for health/safety of relevant employees during, and immediately after, the pregnancy. The Act of 1994 gives a fundamental right to leave with continuity of service preserved and the right to return to the same job or a job no less favourable than that held prior to the taking of the leave. The Act of 2004 makes significant improvements to previous maternity protection legislation such as providing for leave for a male employee in certain circumstances.

Adoptive Leave Acts 1995 and 2005

These Acts provide for leave from employment principally by the adopting mother and a right for her to return to work following such leave. In certain circumstances, there is also a right for the adopting father.

Organisation of Working Time Act 1997

This Act regulates a variety of employment conditions including maximum working hours, night work, shift work, annual and public holiday leave and daily and weekly rest breaks. The Act is a piece of health and safety legislation in that its effect is to prevent people from working too hard. There are, however, a great many employees excluded from the 48 hour per week rule such as doctors, nurses and the self-employed.

Employment Equality Act 1998

This Act prohibits discrimination on nine specific grounds, *viz.* gender, marital status, family status, age, race, religion, disability, sexual orientation and membership of the Traveller community. The Act also prohibits harassment and sexual harassment. This Act must be read in the light of the Equality Act 2004, which amends it by providing for extension of the age provisions of that Act to people under the school leaving age (from 16) and those over 65 years. The Act of 2004 also amends the Equal Status Act 2000 by extending the definition of sexual harassment and shifting the burden of proof from the complainant to the respondent and by amending the economic defence for employers regarding the provision of facilities in order that they might employ disabled employees.

Safety, Health and Welfare at Work Act 2005

This Act repealed and replaced the Safety, Health and Welfare at Work Act 1989. The Act of 2005 makes further provision for the safety, health and welfare of persons at work. The Act clarifies and enhances the responsibilities of employers, self-employed, employees and various other parties in relation to health and safety at work. The Act sets out in some detail the role and functions of the Health and Safety Authority and provides for a range of enforcement measures and penalties that may be applied for breach of the provisions of the Act.

Parental Leave Act 1998 and the Parental Leave (Amendment) Act 2005

These Acts provide for a period of unpaid leave for parents to care for their children and for a limited right to paid *force majeure* leave in circumstances of serious/emergency family illness. Any leave periods taken under the Act do not break continuity of service. An employee who avails of the unpaid leave under the Act is entitled to come back to a job with no less favourable terms and conditions. It is not subsidised by the State and is thus a type of middle class relief.

National Minimum Wage Act 2000

This Act, as the title suggests, provides for an enforceable national minimum wage.

Carers' Leave Act 2001

This Act allows employees to avail of temporary unpaid carer's leave to enable them personally to look after a disabled, aged or infirm person, usually a family member or relative. Any leave periods, which can be substantial, taken under the Act, do not break continuity of service. An employee who avails of the leave is entitled to come back to a job with no less favourable terms and conditions. It is not subsidised by the State and is a type of middle class relief.

Protection of Employees (Part-Time Work) Act 2001

This Act, which replaced the Worker Protection (Regular Part-Time Employees) Act 1991, provides that part-time workers may not be treated less favourably than full-time workers. The Act prohibits discrimination or dismissal of an employee on the basis of his/her part-time status. It has the effect of bringing part-time employees under the protection of the most important pieces of legislation.

Protection of Employees (Fixed-Term Work) Act 2003

This Act is an important piece of legislation. Before its enactment, it was possible for employers to structure their employee relations in such a way as to contract out of the legislation. This Act allows for an employee to gain the protection of employment legislation generally where there have been a series of fixed-term contracts.

The European Communities (Protection of Employees on Transfer of Undertakings) Regulations 2003

This legislation applies to any transfer of an undertaking, business or part of a business from one employer to another employer. Employees' rights and entitlements are protected during and after this transfer. This legislation essentially complements the Unfair Dismissal Act in that it prevents employers from implementing dismissals by reason of the transfer. Whereas it is not appropriate to lay workers off because the business is being bought out, this may, however, be done by agreement. The legislation sets up a very limited redress procedure. Further, there is an obligation on employers to inform and consult with affected employees and where there is no or insufficient or inadequate consultation with employees prior to the transfer, a complaint may be made to the Rights Commissioner.

Employees (Provision of Information and Consultation) Act 2006

This Act implements Directive 2002/14/EC and provides for the establishment of arrangements for informing and consulting employees and from March 23, 2007 in the case of undertakings with at least 150 employees and from March 23, 2008 for undertakings with at least 50 employees. Under this Act employers are obliged to have in place an information and consultation forum to provide information on such matters as recent and probable development of the undertaking's activities and economic situation, the situation, structure and probable development of employment within the undertaking and on any anticipatory measures envisaged, in particular where there is a threat to employment, on decisions likely to lead to substantial changes in work organisation or in the contractual relations including those covered in the transfer of undertakings legislation. It also implements Art.3(2) of Directive 2004/23/EC on the approximation of the laws of the Member States relating to the safeguarding of employees' rights in the event of transfers of undertakings, businesses or parts thereof.

TERMS OF EMPLOYMENT: MINIMUM NOTICE AND TERMS OF EMPLOYMENT ACT 1973

This Act, which came into operation on September 1, 1973, obliges an employer to give a minimum period of notice in order to lawfully terminate the employment of those employees with the qualifying service period (see s.4(2)). An employee may waive their right to notice (see s.7). It is unclear whether the employee has a right to refuse to accept wages in lieu of notice as the Act does not provide a right to give wages in lieu of notice but rather states that there is nothing in the Act which shall operate to prevent an employee from *accepting* payment in lieu of notice.

The requisite notice periods, which are calculated on the basis of service, are as follows:

a) if the employee has been in the continuous service of his employer for less than two years—one week;

b) if the employee has been in the continuous service of his employer for two years or more, but less than five years—two weeks;

c) if the employee has been in the continuous service of his employer for five years or more, but less than 10 years—four weeks;

d) if the employee has been in the continuous service of his employer for 10 years or more, but less than 15 years—six weeks;

(e) if the employee has been in the continuous service of his employer for 15 years or more—eight weeks.

The elements of "notice" which fall for consideration are the notice period itself, the certainty of notice, the sufficiency of the notice period, whether notice can be unilaterally withdrawn, what is to happen if notice is given during a "lay off" period, whether minimum notice can be offset against an employee's holidays, what rights has an employee during the notice period and what rights has the employer to receive notice.

Excluded Employees

There is a qualifying service period of 13 weeks and thus employees with less than 13 weeks' service are excluded (see s.4). The Act states that employees who are normally expected to work 18 hours per week are excluded. However, notwithstanding this, the Act now applies to all part-time employees regardless of the number of hours worked (see s.8 of the Protection of Employees (Part-Time Work) Act 2001). Also excluded are: employees who are members of the employer's family; employees who are a member of the employer's household and whose place of employment is a private dwelling-house or a farm in or on which both the employee and the employer reside; employees of the Civil Service; those employed as a member of the Permanent Defence Forces; those employed as a member of An Garda Síochána; and those employed under an employment agreement pursuant to s.3, Pt II or Pt IV of the Merchant Shipping Act 1894. (On the exclusion in respect of employment under the Merchant Shipping Act 1894, see *Down v B & I Line* (M1426/1989) and *McAuley v B & I Line* (M976/1991)).

An employee who has been constructively dismissed is not entitled to claim under this Act (see *Halal Meat Packers (Ballyhaunis) Ltd v Employment Appeals Tribunal* ([1990] E.L.R. 49, 59)). Neither does the Act affect the right of any employer or employee to terminate a contract of employment without notice because of misconduct by the other party (see *Lennon v Bredin* (M160/1978) and *Creed v KMP Co-op Society Ltd* (UD 187/1990 (reported at [1991] E.L.R. 140)).

The Notice Period

The notice period will either be expressed or implied into the employment contract. The notice required by the Act is a minimum period of notice. If the notice period specified in the contract is greater, then the greater period applies over the statutory period. However, see *Benson v Switzers Ltd* (M850/1984), where the EAT decided the claimant was contractually entitled to three months' notice and, in awarding her compensation under the Act, awarded her the equivalent of three months' salary. Breach of a contractual notice period cannot be enforced under the Act. Rather it must be pursued through an action in the courts under the law of contract (see *Jameson v M.C.W Ltd* (M878/1983)).

Certainty of the Notice Period

The notice must be certain. It is not enough simply to notify an employee that his or her employment will be terminated at some date in the future. There must be precision of date and time (see *Bolands Ltd v*

Ward ([1988] I.L.R.M. 382) and *Waterford Multiport Ltd v Fagan* ([1999] E.L.R. 185)).

Sufficiency of the Notice Period

In *Supple v Period Properties Ltd* (MN609/2001), the claimant, who was entitled to one week's notice, received notice of dismissal on Monday due to expire on Friday. The EAT held that the notice entitlement was five working days, which constituted the statutory entitlement in that case of one week.

Withdrawal of Notice

In *Gallagher v O'Mahoney* (M20/1980) and *O'Looney v Roderick Hogan & Associates* (M2538/1987), it was held that notice, once given, cannot be unilaterally withdrawn by either the employee or the employer.

Rights during the Notice Period

An employee has rights during the period of notice. Thus, an employee should be paid by his employer in respect of any time during his normal working hours when he is ready and willing to work, even if no work is provided for him by his employer (s.5). Where an employee, who is temporarily "laid-off" and whilst on lay-off, is given notice of termination or redundancy, that employee is entitled to be paid during that period of notice. See *Foley v Irish Leathers Ltd* ([1986] I.R. 177) (*sub nom. Irish Leathers Ltd v Minister for Labour*), where the company contended that because the claimant was on a lay-off, he was not in a position to suffer "loss" and was, therefore, not entitled under the Act to be paid during the notice period. This argument was not accepted by the EAT whose decision was upheld by the High Court.

Can minimum notice be offset against an employee's holidays?

The position as to whether the employer is entitled to offset the claimant's minimum notice against his or her holiday entitlement is somewhat confused. Some decisions such as *Kelly v Michael Amber Ltd* (M409/1979), *Buckley v D. & E. Fitzgibbon Ltd* (M808/1986) and *McQuinn v Kennedy* (UD 548/1988) have held that the employer is so entitled, whereas others such as *Maher v Ashton Tinbox Ireland Ltd* (M4720/1986) and *Roche v United Yeast Co. Ltd* (UD 822/1987) have held to the contrary.

Rights of the employer to receive notice

An employer has a right to receive notice of an employee's intention to terminate his/her contract of employment. Under s.12 of the Redundancy Payments Act 1967, an employer is entitled to not less than one week's notice from an employee who has been in his continuous employment for 13 weeks (see *Leopard Security Ltd v Campbell* MN1874/1996 ([1997] E.L.R. 227) and *Murphy v Coogan* MN642/2001). However, the EAT's decisions are declaratory in nature as it has no power to award any compensation to an employer.

Redress

Any dispute arising under this Act (other than a dispute arising under s.9 regarding failure of an employer to furnish written terms) is referred to the EAT, whose decision is final and conclusive, with an appeal to the High Court only on a point of law.

The EAT may award to the employee compensation for any loss sustained by him/her by reason of the default of the employer. Thus, a breach of an employee's right to notice *per se* does not give rise to compensation. Actual loss must have been sustained by an employee because of the failure (see, for example, *Leopard Security v Campbell* ([1997] E.L.R. 227), *McLoughlin v D.N.U. Ltd* (M744/1987) and *Irish Shipping Ltd v Byrne* ([1987] I.R. 468)).

(Note: The First Schedule of this Act contains a Schedule for Computation of Continuous Service. This is very important for almost all employment legislation which depends on the concept of continuous service. The schedule has a presumption against a break of continuity in service.)

TERMS OF EMPLOYMENT: TERMS OF EMPLOYMENT (INFORMATION) ACT 1994

This Act was enacted to implement the provisions of Council Directive 91/533/EEC and came into operation on May 16, 1994. Section 3 of the Act, in essence, puts an obligation on an employer to inform employees of the main terms and conditions applicable to the contract or employment relationship within two months of commencement of the employment. The Act, like the Directive, stops short of imposing an obligation on employers to provide employees with a written contract of employment. What is required is a statement of the "essential aspects" or terms of the contract (see *System Floors (UK) v Daniel* ([1982]

I.C.R. 54 at 58)). If changes are made in the particulars of the terms of employment, these changes must be notified to the employee in writing within one month after the changes take effect.

Excluded Employees

Employees who are normally expected to work for less than eight hours a week were excluded from the Act. However, by virtue of s.8 of the Protection of Employees (Part-Time Work) Act 2001, the Act now applies to all part-time employees regardless of the number of hours worked. Employees who have been in employment for less than one month are excluded and it is permissible to exclude employment relationships that are casual where this is justified by objective considerations.

Particulars that must be supplied

The written statement that an employer is required to provide must contain the following particulars:

(a) the full names of the employer and the employee;

(b) the address of the employer in the State or, where appropriate, the address of the principal place of the relevant business of the employer in the State or the registered office;

(c) the place of work or, where there is no fixed or main place of work, a statement specifying that the employee is required or permitted to work at various places;

(d) the title of the job or nature of the work for which the employee is employed;

(e) the date of commencement of the contract of employment;

(f) in the case of a temporary contract of employment, the expected duration thereof or, if the contract of employment is for a fixed term, the date on which the contract expires;

(g) the rate or method of calculation of the employee's remuneration and the pay reference period for the purposes of the National Minimum Wage Act 2000;

(ga) that the employee may request from the employer a written statement of the employee's average hourly rate of pay for any pay reference period;

(h) the length of the intervals between the times at which remuneration is paid, whether a week, a month or any other interval;

(i) any terms or conditions relating to hours of work (including overtime);

(j) any terms or conditions relating to paid leave (other than paid sick leave);

(k) any terms or conditions relating to:
   (i) incapacity for work due to sickness or injury and paid sick leave, and
   (ii) pensions and pension schemes;

(l) the period of notice which the employee is required to give and entitled to receive or the method for determining such periods of notice;

(m) a reference to any collective agreements which directly affect the terms and conditions of the employee's employment.

The particulars specified in paragraphs (g), (h), (i), (j), (k) and (l) may be given to the employee in the form of a reference to provisions of statutes or instruments made under statute or of any other laws or of any administrative provisions or collective agreements.

Where employees are assigned to work abroad for a period of not less than one month, an employer must provide the complete written statement required by s.3 before the employee's departure.

Where an existing employee makes a requirement of his/her employer to furnish a written statement of particulars, the employer must do so within two months of the date of the request (see *Murphy v Tesco Ireland Ltd* (TE7/1999) and s.6 of the Act).

Redress

An employee may refer a complaint in the first instance to a Rights Commissioner, who is given power, *inter alia*, to correct any inaccuracies or omissions in the statement of particulars but who, however, has no power to adjudicate on terms of employment or to invent particulars or terms of employment which the contract is not required to contain or which have not been agreed (*England v British Telecommunications* ([1993] I.C.R. 644)). Redress may be such compensation as is just and equitable in all the circumstances up to a maximum of four weeks' remuneration and such circumstances will include whether the claimant was "unduly prejudiced" by the failure to provide the written statement (see *Archbold v CMC (Ireland) Ltd* (TE05/ 2003)). Either party may appeal to the EAT, with a further appeal on a point of law to the High Court. In the event of an employer not complying with a recommendation of a Rights Commissioner, the matter may be brought before the EAT.

WORKING TIME AND HOLIDAYS: THE ORGANISATION OF WORKING TIME ACT 1997

The Act, which came into operation on September 30, 1997, transposes into Irish law Council Directive 93/104/EC, concerning certain aspects of the organisation of working time. There is no qualifying service period.

The key provisions of the Act deal with maximum working hours, rest breaks, overtime, zero hour contracts, double employments and holiday entitlements. There is also an entitlement to the payment for any holidays or public holiday compensation owed to an employee at the time of cessation of employment.

- The maximum average net weekly working time is not to exceed 48 hours;
- There must be a daily rest break of 11 consecutive hours;
- There must be rest breaks while at work;
- There must be a weekly rest break of 24 consecutive hours;
- The maximum average night working is not to exceed eight hours.

Where a collective agreement provides for an average working week of more than 48 hours, each employee covered must be named in the agreement and each such employee must have given an informed consent in writing to such an agreement being entered into in relation to that employee. The Labour Court must approve such a collective agreement.

The Act applies to public and private sectors. The Act may be contravened but only where the contravention can be objectively justified such as for technical reasons or reasons concerning the organisation of work, *i.e.* seasonal nature of the work, and there must first be consultation with the employees concerned.

There is an exemption in the Act from the daily and weekly rest provisions in respect of an employee each time he or she changes shift and an employee whose work involves periods of work spread out over the day. There is a further exemption in respect of the working time provisions, without prejudice to the employee's entitlement to compensatory rest in exceptional or emergency circumstances.

Certain specified activities are exempted. These specified activities are:

- An activity in which the employee is regularly required by the employer to travel distances of significant length, either from his or her home to the workplace or from one workplace to another workplace.
- An activity of a security or surveillance nature, the purpose of which is to protect persons or property and which requires the continuous presence of the employee at a particular place or places, and, in particular, the activities of a security guard, caretaker or security firm.
- An activity falling within a sector of the economy or in the public service—
  (a) in which it is foreseeable that the rate at which production or the provision of services, as the case may be, takes place will vary significantly from time to time; or
  (b) the nature of which is such that employees are directly involved in ensuring the continuity of production or the provision of services, as the case may be.

  and, in particular, any of the following activities:
- The provision of services relating to the reception, treatment or care of persons in a residential institution, hospital or similar establishment.
- The provision of services at a harbour or airport.
- Production in the press, radio, television, cinematographic, postal or telecommunications industries.
- The provision of ambulance, fire and civil protection services.
- The production, transmission or distribution of gas, water or electricity.

- The collection of household refuse or the operation of an incineration plant.
- Any industrial activity in which work cannot, by reason of considerations of a technical nature, be interrupted.
- Research and development.
- Agriculture.
- Tourism.

The exemptions only apply if the employee is engaged "wholly or mainly" in carrying on or performing the duties of the activity concerned or if the employee is either a special category night worker within the meaning of the Act or falls within a class of employee under the Industrial Relations Acts 1946 to 2004. If an employee is not entitled, by reason of this exemption, to the rest period and break periods referred to in the Act, the employer must ensure that the employee has available a rest period and break that, in all the circumstances, can reasonably be regarded as equivalent. Where it is not possible for an employer to ensure that the employees avail of the minimum rest to which they are entitled, then the employer must make such arrangements as will compensate the employee save that that compensation cannot be of monetary or material benefit. This compensation must take the form of provision of a benefit which improves the physical conditions under which the employees work or the amenities or services available to the employees while at work, such as enhanced environmental conditions to accommodate regular long periods of attendance at work, refreshment facilities, recreational and reading material, appropriate facilities/amenities such as television, radio and music, alleviating monotonous work or isolation, transport to and from work where appropriate. The measures listed are not exhaustive and are for illustrative purposes only. Employers should consider other measures that might be more relevant to their circumstances.

An employer cannot require an employee, to whom the exemption applies, to work during a shift or other period of work of more than six hours' duration without allowing the employee a break of such duration as the employer determines. In determining the duration of this break, the employer must have regard to the need to protect and secure the health, safety and comfort of the employee and to the general principles concerning the prevention and avoidance of risk at the workplace. In *The Tribune Printing & Publishing Group v Graphical Print & Media Union* (DWT6 and 7/2004), the Labour Court held that an employer was under a positive duty to ensure that employees received their rest breaks and that "merely stating that employees could take rest breaks if they wished and not putting in place proper procedures to ensure that the employee receives those breaks, thus protecting his health and safety, does not discharge that duty."

Where an employee is required to work on a Sunday, there is an entitlement to a premium payment for the work which may consist of a payment or time off in lieu or a combination of both (see *Group 4 Securitas v SIPTU* (DWT 6/1999) and *Campbell Catering Ltd v SIPTU* (DWT 35/2000)).

Excluded Employees

The Act does not apply to the following categories of employee:

- a member of An Garda Síochána or the Defence Forces.
- a person engaged in sea fishing, other work at sea or the activities of a doctor in training.
- a person who is employed by a relative and is a member of that relative's household, and whose place of employment is a private dwelling house or a farm in or on which he or she and the relative reside.
- a person, the duration of whose working time (saving any minimum period of such time that is stipulated by the employer) is determined by himself or herself, whether or not provision for the making of such determination by that person is made by his or her contract of employment.

An employee must be notified in advance of the hours which the employer will require the employee to work overtime, subject to unforeseeable circumstances justifying a change in the notified times. The Labour Court has held that an employer is generally obliged to give an employee at least 24 hours' notice of overtime working (see *Anglo Irish Beef Processors v SIPTU* (DWT 19/2000)).

Zero Hour Contracts

Zero hour contracts are arrangements where an employee is either asked to be available for work, without the guarantee of work, or where an employee is informed that there will be work available on a specified day or days. In the event of an employer failing to require an employee to work at least 25 per cent of the contractual time, that employee will be entitled to payment for the said 25 per cent of the contract hours or 15 hours, whichever is less. There is no entitlement to this minimum payment if there is only an "expectation" that employment would be given and the employee must have had advance notice of being required to work or where the contract operates to require the employee to be available for work (see *Ocean Manpower Ltd and the Marine Port v General Workers' Union* ([1998] E.L.R)).

Example: If the employee's contract of employment operates to require the employee to be available for 40 hours in a week, he or she will be entitled to a minimum payment of 10 hours even if not required to work that week. Similarly, if an employee is asked to be available over a four-week period and is not called into work, that employee will be entitled to a minimum payment of 15 hours or 25 per cent of the number of hours worked by another employee doing such work and for such number of hours as the "zero hours" employee would or could have done had he or she been called into work.

Double Employment

Double employment, where the aggregate total of hours worked exceeds what is permitted by the provisions of the Act, is prohibited.

Holiday Entitlements

Although an employer and employee are free to contract as regards holiday entitlements, any such arrangement agreed between the parties must comply with ss.19 and 20 of the Act which provide for a four-week holiday entitlement. The Act sets out the criteria which apply to the times at which annual leave should be granted and to payment for this leave. Although the times at which annual leave is granted are to be determined by the employer, the employer must take into account not only the opportunities for rest and recreation available to the employee but also the need for the employee to reconcile work and any family responsibilities. In addition, the employer must consult with the employee or the trade union of which he or she is a member, not later than one month before the day on which the annual leave (or portion thereof) is due to commence. The legislation allows for the extension of the leave year by an additional six months (see *Royal Liver Assurance Ltd v Macken* ([2002] 4 I.R. 427)).

Holiday entitlements are calculated as follows:

(a) Four working weeks in a leave year in which he or she works at least 1,365 hours (unless it is a leave year in which he or she changes employment);

(b) one-third of a working week for each month in the leave year in which he or she works at least 117 hours; or

(c) 8 per cent of the hours he or she works in a leave year (but subject to a maximum of four working weeks).

If more than one of the preceding paragraphs is applicable and the period of annual leave, determined in accordance with each, is not identical, the greater period of annual leave applies.

Where an employee is ill on a day of annual leave and furnishes to his or her employer a medical certificate, that day shall not be regarded as a day of annual leave.

The annual leave of an employee who works eight months or more in a leave year should include an unbroken period of two weeks.

Public Holiday Entitlements

Public holidays are designated in this Act and the criteria which shall apply to public holiday entitlements are set out in s.21. The qualifying period is at least 40 hours' work during the five weeks before the public holiday. An employee will be entitled to a public holiday even though that employee is not rostered to work a public holiday. Where an employee is entitled to a public holiday, he may either have a paid day off on that day, a paid day off within a month of that day, an additional day of annual leave or an additional day's pay.

Redress

A complaint should be made to the Rights Commissioner not later than six months, beginning on the date of the contravention to which the complaint relates. The Rights Commissioner may require the employer to comply with the relevant provisions, or to pay compensation of such amount (if any) as is just and equitable having regard to all the circumstances, up to a maximum of two years' remuneration. An appeal, which must be made within six weeks of the date on which the decision was communicated to the party, lies from a decision of a Rights Commissioner to the Labour Court, with a further right of appeal on a point of law only to the High Court. Where an employer fails to implement a decision of the Rights Commissioner under the Act, the Labour Court shall make a determination to the like effect as the original decision without hearing the employer concerned.

WAGES

The Payment of Wages Act 1991 and The National Minimum Wage Act 2000 are the enactments that impact on wages.

The Payment of Wages Act 1991

This Act, which came into operation on January 1, 1992, provides for matters related to the payment of wages. There is no qualifying service period or minimum hours threshold. The definition of "employee" makes it clear that all persons employed by or under the State are included.

There are three basic rights enshrined in this Act. These are:

(1) The right of every employee to a readily negotiable mode of wage payment.
(2) The right of every employee to protection against unlawful deductions.
(3) The right of every employee to a written statement of wages and any deductions therefrom.

The Act, however, does not impose a mode of wage payment, other than cash, on an employee who has been entitled up to the implementation of the Act to wages in cash.

"Wages" is defined as any sums payable to the employee by the employer in connection with his employment, including any fee, bonus or commission, any holiday, sick or maternity pay, any other emolument referable to the employment, and any sum payable to the employee upon the termination by the employer of his contract of employment, without his having given to the employee the appropriate prior notice of the termination, being a sum paid in lieu of the giving of such notice. Where employees do not receive from the outset what is "properly payable" to them, then this could amount to a deduction within the meaning of the Act (see *Sullivan v Department of Education* ([1998] E.L.R. 217)). The definition of "wages" does not include: any payment in respect of expenses incurred by the employee in carrying out his employment; any payment by way of a pension, allowance or gratuity in connection with the death, or the retirement or resignation from his employment of the employee or as compensation for loss of office;

any payment referable to the employee's redundancy; any payment to the employee otherwise than in his capacity as an employee; or any payment in kind or benefit in kind.

Section 4 of the Act imposes on employers an obligation to give to each employee a written statement of wages and deductions. The statement must be given to the employee at the time of wage payment, except in the case of payment by credit transfer, when the statement should be given as soon as possible thereafter. An employer is prohibited under the Act from making a deduction or receiving any payment unless the deduction or payment is required by statute, such as PAYE and PRSI or it is authorised by a term in the contract of employment, such as a pension contribution or it is a deduction to which the employee has consented in writing, such as a trade union subscription (see s.5 and *Potter v Hunt Contracts Ltd* ([1992] I.R.L.R.108), a decision of English EAT on a similar provision in the English equivalent of this Act). The consent of the employee must be an informed consent (see *Hurley v Royal Yacht Club* ([1997] E.L.R. 225)). All other deductions are prohibited save those such as deductions or payments, the purpose of which is the reimbursement of the employer (see *Beaumont Hospital v McNally* (PN29/1996)). Where a deduction is made in respect of either goods or services supplied by the employer which are necessary to the employment, such as an employee's contribution towards the purchase or cleaning of work clothes or the supply of transport to work by the employer or where a deduction is made in respect of any act or omission of the employee, the amount deducted must be fair and reasonable, having regard to all the circumstances including the amount of the wages of the employee in question (see *Riley v Joseph Frisby Ltd* ([1982] I.R.L.R. 479)). A failure to pay wage could be regarded as 100 per cent deduction.

Redress

A complaint regarding unlawful deductions goes at first instance to a Rights Commissioner with a right of appeal to the EAT and a further appeal on a point of law only to the High Court, whose decision is "final and conclusive" (ss.6 and 7). Section 8 provides for the enforcement of a decision of a Rights Commissioner or a determination of the EAT as if it were an order of the Circuit Court.

The National Minimum Wage Act 2000

This Act, which went into operation on April 1, 2000, provides the legislative framework for the introduction of a national minimum hourly rate of pay. An employee under the age of 18 years must be paid at an hourly rate of pay that, on average, is not less than 70 per cent of the national minimum hourly rate (s.14). The Act also provides for the enforcement and recovery of wages and the imposition of penalties for breaches of the Act. Provisions in any agreement whatsoever to pay less than the national minimum hourly rate of pay are void (s.7). (See *Fitzgerald v Pat the Baker* ([1999] E.L.R. 227)).

Excluded Employees

Excluded from the Act are employees who are the spouse, father, mother, grandfather, grandmother, stepfather, stepmother, son, daughter, stepson, stepdaughter, grandson, granddaughter, brother, sister, half-brother or half-sister of an employer or an apprentice within the meaning of or under the Industrial Training Act 1967, or the Labour Services Act 1987 (see s.5). Additionally, the Labour Court may grant an employer a temporary exemption from paying the national minimum hourly rate of pay to an employee or to a number of employees in circumstances where the employer is unable to pay, and that employer would likely otherwise have to lay off or dismiss the employees concerned, and the majority of employees affected have consented (see s.41).

Calculating the Hourly Rate

Section 19 contains a formula for calculating the average hourly rate of pay and provides that reckonable components include basic salary, shift premium, piece and incentive rates, commission and bonuses which are productivity related, the monetary value of board and lodgings, the amount of any service charge distributed to the employee through the payroll and any payments under s.18 of the Organisation of Working Time Act 1997 (zero hour protection). Non-reckonable components are: overtime premium, call-out premium, service pay, unsocial hours premium, tips or gratuities paid through the payroll, public holiday premium, Saturday and Sunday premiums when such days are worked, allowances for special or additional duties, including those of a post responsibility, expenses such as travel allowance, subsistence allowance, tool allowance and clothing allowance, on-call or standby allowance, sick pay, holiday pay, payment for health and safety leave under the Maternity Protection Act 1994, or pay in lieu of notice, any payment by way of an allowance or gratuity in connection with the retirement or resignation of the employee or as compensation for loss of office, pension contributions paid by the employer on behalf of the employee, any payment referable to the employee's redundancy, any payment-in-kind or benefit-in-kind (except board with lodgings), any payment to the employee otherwise than in his or her capacity as an employee, any payment representing compensation for the employee, such as for injury or loss of tools and equipment, an amount of any award under a staff suggestion scheme and any loan by the employer to the employee, other than an advance payment.

Redress

Redress is sought from a Rights Commissioner within six months or such longer period, not exceeding 12 months, as the Rights Commissioner may allow. The Rights Commissioner may order the payment of arrears of pay owed to the employee in accordance with the Act and may also award reasonable expenses to a successful employee. There is a right of appeal within six weeks to the Labour Court, with a further right of appeal to the High Court on a point of law only (see s.27). Civil proceedings may be instituted by an employee as an alternative remedy, or the relevant government minister may institute civil proceedings on behalf of an employee in appropriate circumstances (see s.39).

TRANSFER OF UNDERTAKINGS AND EMPLOYER'S INSOLVENCY

Protection of Employees (Employers' Insolvency) Act 1984

This Act, which came into operation on November 30, 1984, implements two European Council Directives (see 80/987/EEC and 2002/74/EC) and places obligations on the State to ensure that a fund is available from which employees can claim payment of debts, arising from the employment relationship, which have not been paid because of their employer's insolvency. This fund is known as the "Social Insurance Fund". The debts for which the employee can claim payment under the Act include up to eight weeks' arrears of normal pay, sick pay and accrued holiday pay, subject to a weekly maximum (currently €507.90). A claim can also be made for amounts due to the employee arising from proceedings under worker protection legislation.

The purpose of the Act is to ensure a minimum level of protection for employees who have suffered as a result of their employer's insolvency (see Joined Cases C–9/90 and 9/90 *Francovich and Bonifaci v Italian Republic* [1991] E.C.R. I-5357). The *Francovich* case also established that employees who suffer loss because of a State's failure under the Act may claim damages in their national courts. There is also an obligation under the Act on the State to protect the interests of workers in relation to pension schemes.

Employees protected by the Act are defined as those in employment which is insurable for all benefits under the Social Welfare Acts, namely "employment such that a person, over the age of 16 years and under pensionable age, employed therein would be an employed contributor" (see *Kenny v Minister for Enterprise, Trade and Employment* ([1999] E.L.R. 163)). The benefits provided by the Act are now extended to employees who have attained the age of 66 years and who are in employment which, but for the age of the employees, would be insurable for all benefits under the Social Welfare Acts and by virtue of s.8 of the Protection of Employees (Part-Time Work) Act 2001, the benefits of the Act are extended to all part-time employees.

Importantly, the Act of 1984 also standardises the number of normal working hours required by an employee to qualify for rights under employment legislation — such as the Redundancy Payments Act 1967, the Minimum Notice and Terms of Employment Act 1973 and the Unfair Dismissals Act 1977 — at 18 hours a week, provided those employees satisfy the other requirements in the Acts.

The Act deems the employer to be insolvent in some situations in which the employer would not be deemed insolvent commercially or for the purposes of other legal rules. This is important where business has ceased but no steps are taken to declare the employer insolvent.

The main rights conferred on affected employees on the insolvency of the employer are contained in s.6 and are as follows: that the applicant will be paid from the Social Insurance Fund any amount which an employer is required to pay, such as any unpaid normal weekly remuneration; any remuneration due to the employee in lieu of the statutory notice period; any holiday pay in respect of a period or periods of holiday not exceeding eight weeks in all, and to which the applicant became entitled during the relevant period; any amount which an employer is required to pay by virtue of employee protection legislation. All of these amounts must have been due to the employee on the date of insolvency and for a "relevant period". As regards "the relevant period", see *Meade v Irish Ispat Ltd* (I 1/2002), where the Tribunal held that it was not permitted "to look further back than to eighteen months prior to the liquidation".

A claim may be made for up to eight weeks' arrears of "normal weekly remuneration". Claims may be paid, up to a maximum amount, from the Social Insurance Fund where an insolvent employer has failed to pay contributions in accordance with an occupational pension scheme or Personal Retirement Savings Account (see s.7 and *Re Cavan Rubber Ltd* ([1992] E.L.R.79)).

Redress

Complaints which must be made within six weeks may be made to the EAT by employees or persons acting on behalf of a pension scheme, where a minister fails to make a payment or where the payment is considered to be less than the amount which should have been paid. Where the complainant is an employee, complaints can relate only to claims concerning arrears of remuneration, sick pay and holiday pay. The EAT does not have the power to award costs (see *Re Cavan Rubber Ltd* ([1992] E.L.R. 79 at 83)). It would appear that the decision of the EAT is final and conclusive save that appeals can be made to the High Court on a question of law.

The European Communities (Protection of Employees on Transfer of Undertakings) Regulations 2003

This Regulation seeks to ensure that, in any transfer of a business, undertaking or part thereof, the employment of the existing workers is preserved or, if their employment terminates by reason of the transfer, that their rights arising out of that termination are effectively safeguarded. Employees dismissed before the transfer must be considered as still employed by the undertaking on the date of the transfer (see Case 101/87 *P Bork International A/S v Foreningen af Arbeijdsledere i Danmark* [1988] E.C.R. 3057). The legislation also imposes significant information and consultation obligations on transferor employers. The Regulations apply to all entities, public or private, which carry on economic activities irrespective of whether they operated with a view to profit or not. The Regulations do not apply to sea-going vessels. A person cannot agree to exclude or limit the application of the regulations and any provision which purports to so do will be void. Further, a provision in any agreement which is or becomes less favourable regarding entitlements conferred on the employee by these Regulations, shall be deemed to be modified so as not to be less favourable.

Where the business of the employer transfers to another person, no matter how the transfer occurs, the rights and obligations of that employer—the transferor—arising from a contract of employment or from an employment relationship existing on the date of a transfer shall, by reason of such transfer, be transferred to the transferee—the new employer. It matters not whether a business is bought out or taken over as a going concern, the person taking on the business is deemed to take all the employees with the business (see, for example, *Mulqueen v Verit Hotel and Leisure (Ireland) Ltd* [1993] E.L.R. 162). The common law rule that the contract of employment automatically terminates on the sale of a business has been replaced as a result of this legislation (see Reg.4 and *Nokes v Doncaster Amalgamated Collieries Ltd* ([1940] A.C. 1014) on the English equivalent of this provision). The transferee—the new employer—must continue to observe the terms and conditions agreed in any collective agreement on the same terms until the date of termination or expiry of the collective agreement or the entry into force or application of another collective agreement (see *Beckmann v Dynamco Whicheloe Macfarlane Ltd, nyr*, Case C–164/00; [2002] I.R.L.R. 578, June 4, 2002 and *Martin v South Bank University* Case C–4/01; [2004] I.R.L.R. 74).

The transfer of an undertaking, business or part of a business, shall not in itself constitute grounds for dismissal by the transferor or the transferee. However, where a dismissal is for economic, technical or organisational reasons entailing changes in the work-force, it is permissible. If a contract of employment or an employment relationship is terminated because a transfer involves a substantial change in working conditions to the detriment of the employee, the employer shall be regarded as having been responsible for termination of the contract of employment or of the employment relationship (see *Powell and McHugh v Bewleys Manufacturing Ltd* ([1990] E.L.R. 68) and *Trafford v Sharpe & Fisher (Building Supplies) Ltd* ([1994] I.R.L.R. 325)).

When does a transfer of undertakings occur?

Wherever, in the context of contractual relations, there is a change in the natural or legal person who incurs the obligations of an employer towards the employees of the undertaking, a transfer occurs (see, in particular, Joined Cases C–171/94 and 172/94 *Merck and Neuhuys v Ford Motors Belgium SA* [1996] E.C.R. I-1253). A transfer occurs not only where there is a sale of an undertaking but also where there is a merger either by acquisition or by formation of a new company. Essentially, the transferee takes over significant assets or a major part of the workforce. The legislation covers situations where part of the business is contracted out (Case C–48/94 *Rygaard v Stro Molle Akustik SA* [1995] E.C.R. I-2745 and *Suzen* [1997] E.C.R. 1-1259). In *Blaney v Vanguard Plastics Ireland Ltd* (UD 271/2000), the Tribunal ruled that the Regulations applied to a transfer of a business "unless the company involved is the subject to a compulsory court-ordered winding up and has been adjudged insolvent by a competent judicial authority." This determination was upheld in the Circuit Court (unreported, May 22, 2001). However, if the main reason for the institution of bankruptcy or insolvency proceedings is the evasion of the employer's obligations under the Regulations, then the Regulations will apply. The Regulations will apply to transfers effected during procedures prior to a winding-up, such as transfers effected by a receiver, an examiner or a provisional liquidator (see, for example, *Mythen v Employment Appeals Tribunal* [1990] 1 I.R. 98 and *Blaney*).

The decisive criterion for establishing the existence of a transfer is whether the economic entity in question retains its identity (see, in particular, Case 24/85 *Spijkers v Gebroeders Benedik Abbatoir CV* [1986] E.C.R. 1119 and Case C–29/91 *Dr Sophie Redmond Stichting v Bartol* [1992] E.C.R. I-3189). In the latter case, the European Court of Justice went on to list a number of elements characterising a transaction which the national court or tribunal must keep in mind when determining whether the entity in question had retained its identity. These include:

- the type of undertaking or business concerned;
- whether its tangible and/or intangible assets are transferred;
- whether its customers and/or employees are transferred; and
- the degree of similarity between activities carried on before and after the transaction.

These elements, the court emphasised, were merely single factors in the overall assessment, which must be made and could not be considered in isolation.

Who is a "transferor"?

A "transferor" is defined in the legislation as meaning any natural or legal person who, by reason of a legal transfer or merger, ceases to be or becomes the employer in respect of the undertaking, business or part of the business so transferred.

Who is a "transferee?
A "transferee" is defined as any natural or legal person who, by reason of a transfer within the meaning of these Regulations, becomes the employer in respect of the undertaking, business or part of the undertaking or business.

The Duty to Inform Workers of a Proposed Transfer of Undertakings
The Regulations create a broad duty to inform and a narrower duty to consult with "employee representatives" (Reg.8). The employer must inform the employees affected of:

    (a) the reasons for the transfer;
    (b) the legal, economic and social implications of the transfer for the employees; and
    (c) the measures envisaged in relation to the employees,

and the information shall be given:

    (i) by the transferor to the representatives of his employees in good time before the transfer is carried out, and
    (ii) by the transferee to the representatives of his employees in good time, and in any event before his employees are directly affected by the transfer as regards their conditions of work and employment.

Where there are no representatives of the employees in the undertaking or business of the transferor or, as the case may be, the transferor or transferee, as may be appropriate, shall cause:

    (a) a statement in writing to be given to each employee in the business or undertaking in good time before the transfer is carried out; and
    (b) notices containing the particulars aforesaid to be displayed prominently in good time before the transfer is carried out at positions in the workplaces of the employees where they can be read conveniently by the employees.

See Case C–383/92 *EC Commission v United Kingdom* ([1994] E.C.R. I-2479).

Redress

Regulation 10 provides that an employee or trade union may make a complaint to a Rights Commissioner within six months of the alleged contravention unless the Rights Commissioner is satisfied that failure to present the complaint within that period was due to exceptional circumstances. There is a right of appeal to the EAT (Reg.11) and, thereafter, a right of appeal on a point of law only to the High Court.

Redress may include the employer being required to comply with the Regulations and, for that purpose, to take a specified course of action, or be required to pay to the employee compensation of such amount as is just and equitable in the circumstances, but in the case of a contravention of Reg.8 (the duty to inform and/or consult), not exceeding four weeks' remuneration and, in the case of a contravention of any other Regulation, not exceeding two years' remuneration,

YOUNG WORKERS AND WORKERS OTHER THAN FULL-TIME AND PERMANENT

Protection of Young Persons (Employment) Act 1996

This Act, which came into operation on January 2, 1997, repeals the Protection of Young Persons (Employment) Act 1977, and certain provisions of the Conditions of Employment Act 1936. The Act satisfies Ireland's obligations under Art.32 of the UN Convention on the Rights of the Child (ratified in 1992) and continues to implement ILO Convention No.79 on Night Work by Young People.

The key provisions of the Act, which are in ss.3 and 4, raise the minimum age for normal working from 15 to 16 years. However, 14 and 15-year olds are allowed to work during the school holidays and for a limited amount of time during term time but there are restrictions on the amount of hours and the number of days to be worked. The section also allows the appropriate minister to authorise by licence in individual cases, the employment of a child of 15 to 16 years in cultural, artistic, sports or advertising activities which are not likely to be harmful to the safety, health or development of the child and which are not likely to interfere with the child's attendance at school, vocational guidance or training programmes. The Minister may also, by regulation, authorise likewise for a child over 13 years of age.

The Act imposes duties on an employer in relation to young persons employed by him/her, such as requiring the production of a birth certificate or other satisfactory evidence of the age of the young person, obtaining the written permission of the parent or guardian of the child, and maintaining a register, or other satisfactory record, containing, in relation to every young person or child employed by him/her, *inter alia*, the number of hours worked, the times of same and details of pay. This obligation does not apply in respect of the employment of close relatives of an employer.

An employer is under an obligation not to permit a child employee to do for him or her any form of work on any day on which that child employee has done any form of work for any other employer, except where the aggregate of the periods does not exceed the period for which such an employee could lawfully be employed to do work for one employer on that day.

An abstract of the Act must be displayed at the principal entrances to the premises where young employees work.

It shall be a defence for an employer if he/she can demonstrate to the satisfaction of the court or tribunal that any breach was rendered necessary or reasonably proper by the actual occurrence or the threat or reasonable anticipation of fire, flood, storm, violence, a breakdown of plant or machinery or any other emergency.

Redress
Redress is sought at first instance from the Rights Commissioner. Either party may appeal to the EAT from a recommendation of the Rights Commissioner and there is a further appeal on a point of law only to the High Court. If an employer fails to carry out a determination of the Tribunal within six weeks from the date on which the determination is communicated to the parties, the District Court shall—on application by the parent or guardian of the child or young person concerned, or the trade union of the young person concerned, or Minister—without hearing the employer concerned, make an order directing the employer to carry out the determination in accordance with its terms. The District Court may, if in all the circumstances it considers it appropriate to do so, where the order relates to the payment of compensation, direct the employer concerned to pay to the employee concerned interest on the compensation.

The Protection of Employees (Part-Time Work) Act 2001

This Act, which came into operation on December 20, 2001, seeks to prevent part-time employees being less favourably treated than comparable full-time employees unless objective grounds exist to justify such less favourable treatment. Thus, this Act seeks to provide for the removal of discrimination against part-time workers on the basis of their status as part-time workers (see *Abbott Ireland Ltd v SIPTU* (PTD3/2004)). It applies to part-time workers who have an employment contract or an employment relationship as defined by the law. The Act makes a distinction between a part-time worker and a casual worker. What may not be considered as an objective ground justifying discriminatory treatment in relation to a part-time employee may be considered an objective ground in relation to a casual employee.

In order to determine if there has been a contravention of the Act as a result of the employer engaging in prohibited discriminatory treatment of a part-time worker, it is necessary to have a comparator. A comparator in the context of a part-time employee is generally a full-time employee engaged in like work. However, s.7 of the Act provides that in the absence of a comparable full-time employee in the employment where the part-time employee is employed, the comparator may be drawn from the same industry or sector of employment. As regards "agency workers", they can only compare themselves to comparable employees who are also agency workers. See, however, *Rooney v Diageo Global Supply* ([2004] E.L.R. 133), where the claimant, who was a registered general nurse supplied to the respondent by a licensed employment agency and paid by the agency, was found by the Labour Court to be employed by the respondent under a contract of employment and was thus able to use non-agency workers as comparators.

Who is a part-time employee/worker?
A part-time employee/worker is defined as an employee whose normal hours of work are less than the normal hours of work of a comparable full-time employee.

Section 8 of the Act provides, in general terms, that a part-time employee shall not be treated less favourably than a comparable full-time employee in respect of conditions of employment. Specifically, s.8 of the Act provides that each relevant legislative provision shall apply equally to a part-time employee as to a comparable full-time employee. Up to the enactment of the 2001 Act, part-time employees who worked less than 18 hours per week were excluded from important employment protection statutes such as the Unfair Dismissals Act 1977.

Permissible Discrimination

A part-time employee may, in respect of a particular condition of employment, be treated less favourably than a comparable full-time employee if that treatment can be justified on "objective grounds", *i.e.* grounds other than the employee's status as a part-time worker. The less favourable treatment must also be for the purpose of achieving a legitimate objective of the employer and must be necessary for that purpose (see *Curry v Boxmore Plastics* Ltd (PTD5/2003)). In *Abbott*, the Labour Court held that the "fact that the break given to full-time employees is in line with their entitlements under the Organisation of Working Time Act cannot be used as objective justification for the less favourable treatment of part-time employees. Indeed, the Act is quite clear in what must be justified is not the more favourable treatment of full-time employees, but the less favourable treatment of part-time employees ...". Benefits, accorded to a part-time employee, shall be on the basis of the principle of *pro rata temporis*. However, see *Ennis v Department of Justice, Equality and Law Reform* (PTD1/2004), where the Labour Court upheld a complaint that paying part-time traffic wardens, who worked 50 per cent of the hours of full-time wardens, only 50 per cent of the travel allowance constituted a contravention of s.10 of the Act (see also *Campbell Catering Ltd v SIPTU* (DWT 35/ 2000)). A part-time employee who normally works less than 20 per cent of the normal hours of work of a comparable full-time employee may be treated less favourably in relation to pensions.

Redress

Redress is dealt with in s.14. A complaint may be referred at first instance within six months of the date of contravention to a Rights Commissioner who may, if the complaint is upheld, award compensation subject to a limit of two years' remuneration. An extension of time up to a further 12 months may be granted if the failure to refer the case within six months was due to a "reasonable cause". A decision of a Rights Commissioner may be appealed to the Labour Court within six weeks of the date of the decision, with a further right of appeal on a point of law only to the High Court. Where a decision of a Rights Commissioner has not been carried out by the employer, and an appeal has not been brought, the employee may refer the complaint to the Labour Court and that court, without hearing any evidence, shall make a determination to the like effect as the decision of the Rights Commissioner.

Protection of Employees (Fixed-Term Work) Act 2003

This Act, which came into operation on July 14, 2003, provides for the application of the principle of non-discrimination to fixed-term workers; in other words, such workers may not be treated less favourably than comparable permanent workers. Importantly, the Act also establishes a framework to prevent abuse arising from the use of successive fixed-term employment contracts.

In order to determine if there has been a contravention on the non-discriminatory principle in the Act, it will be necessary to identify a comparator. A comparator in the context of a fixed-term contract employee is generally a permanent employee engaged in like work. The Act itself identifies the comparator group as being a permanent employee employed by the same employer or a permanent employee specified in a collective agreement or a permanent employee employed in the same industry or sector. This is an "either or" test and is not a cumulative one.

Who is a fixed-term employee?

A "fixed-term employee" is defined as a person having a contract of employment entered into directly with an employer, where the end of the contract of employment is determined by an objective condition such as arriving at a specific date, completing a specific task or the occurrence of a specific event (see s.2(1)). Excluded are employees with less than one year's service, employees in initial vocational training relationships or apprenticeship schemes, or employees with a contract of employment which has been concluded within the framework of a specific public or publicly-supported training, integration or vocational retraining programme.

Section 6 provides, in general terms, that a fixed-term employee shall not be treated less favourably than a comparable permanent employee in respect of his or her conditions of employment. However, a fixed-term employee may, in respect of particular conditions of employment, be treated less favourably than a comparable permanent employee if that treatment can be justified on "objective grounds". The objective grounds must be based on considerations other than the status of the employee as a fixed-term contract worker and the less favourable treatment must be for the purpose of achieving a legitimate objective of the employer and must be appropriate and necessary for that purpose. Importantly, where an employee is in his/her third year of continuous employment with an employer or associate employer, that employer may only renew the fixed-term contract once more and for not longer than one year. Additionally, the aggregate duration of such contracts shall not exceed four years where the first contract postdates the Act. If these provisions are infringed, the contract is deemed to be a contract of indefinite duration. However, there is a "let out" if there are objective grounds justifying the infringement.

A fixed-term employee who normally works less than 20 per cent of the normal hours of work of a comparable permanent employee may be treated less favourably in relation to pensions.

The Act imposes an obligation on an employer to inform a fixed-term employee in relation to vacancies to ensure that the employee shall have the same opportunity to secure a permanent position. In so far as is practicable, there is an obligation on an employer to facilitate access by a fixed-term employee to appropriate training opportunities to enhance his or her skills, career development and occupational mobility.

Redress
Section 18 deals with redress and it is identical in its terms to s.14 of the Part-Time Workers Act above.

DEFINITIONS—ESSENTIAL TERMS

In employment law, particularly when dealing with legislative provisions, it is important to know what various words and terms mean. The Acts, either in the interpretation section or elsewhere throughout the Act, give definitions for these words and terms. Definitions may vary somewhat for the purpose of a particular statute, thus, it is important to check out the definition ascribed to a particular word or term in the particular Act in question. Some of the more important terms and a definition of them are as follows:

Contract of Employment: "Contract of employment" means a contract of service or apprenticeship, and any other contract whereby an individual agrees with another person, who is carrying on the business of an employment agency within the meaning of the Employment Agency Act 1971, and is acting in the course of that business, to do or perform personally any work or service for a third person (whether or not the third person is a party to the contract), whether the contract is express or implied and if express, whether it is oral or in writing.

Registered Employment Agreement: "Registered employment agreement" means a registered employment agreement within the meaning of the Industrial Relations Acts 1946–2001.

Collective Agreement: A "collective agreement" means an agreement by or on behalf of an employer on the one hand, and by or on behalf of a body or bodies representative of the employees to whom the agreement relates on the other hand. This definition differs from the definition of collective agreement in s.1(1) of the Anti-Discrimination (Pay) Act 1974, which covered agreements "relating to terms and conditions of employment" which are made "between parties who are or who represent employers and parties who are or represent employees". It also differs somewhat from the definition in s.1(1) of the Protection of Young Persons (Employment) Act 1996 which covers agreements "by or on behalf of an employer on the one hand and by or on behalf of a trade union or trade unions representative of the employees to whom the agreement relates on the other hand".

Employee: Whether under statute or for the purpose of the law of contract, an "employee" is a person who has entered into or works under (or, where the employment has ceased, entered into or worked under) a contract of employment—a contract of services. Under the Acts, a person holding office under, or in the service of the State (including a member of An Garda Síochána or the Defence Forces) or otherwise as a civil servant, within the meaning of the Civil Service Regulation Act 1956, shall be deemed to be an employee employed by the State or Government, as the case may be. An officer or servant of a local authority for the purposes of the Local Government Act 1941 — a harbour authority, a health board or a vocational education committee—shall be deemed to be an employee employed by the authority, board or committee, as the case may be. However, in respect of some of the statutes, members of An Garda Síochána, the Defence Forces or civil servants are excluded. Note: Since 2005, Civil Servants are no longer excluded from the provisions of unfair dismissal legislation.

Permanent Employee: A "permanent employee" means an employee who is not a fixed-term employee.

Part-time Employee: A "part-time employee" means an employee whose normal hours of work are less than the normal hours of work of an employee who is a comparable employee in relation to him or her.

Fixed-term Contract Worker: A "fixed-term employee" means a person having a contract of employment entered into directly with an employer, where the end of the contract of employment concerned is determined by an objective condition such as arriving at a specific date, completing a specific task or the occurrence of a specific event.

Outworker: An "outworker" means an employee who is employed under a contract of service to do work for his or her employer in the employee's own home or in some other place not under the control or management of the employer, being work that consists of the making of a product or the provision of a service specified by the employer.

Child: "Child" means a person who has not reached the age of 16 years.

Young Person: A "young person" means a person who has reached the age of 16 years but has not reached the age of 18 years.

Employer: An "employer" means the person who is liable to pay the wages of the "employee" in respect of the work or service for which the employee is hired. An "employer" is also defined as being the person with whom the employee has entered into or for whom the employee works under (or, where the employment has ceased, entered into or worked under) a contract of employment and who is liable to pay the wages of the individual concerned in respect of the work or service concerned.

Associate Employer: Employers are deemed to be associated if one is a body corporate of which the other (whether directly or indirectly) has control, or both are bodies corporate of which a third person (whether directly or indirectly) has control.

Business: "Business" includes a trade, industry, profession or undertaking, or any activity carried on by a person or body of persons, whether corporate or unincorporated, or by a public or local authority or a Department of State.

Day: A "day" means a period of 24 consecutive hours commencing at midnight.

Week: A "week" means a period of seven consecutive days.

Year: A "year" means any period of 52 weeks.

Working Time: "Working time" means any period during which a person is at work, at the employer's disposal and carrying out his or her activity or duties.

Hours of Work: "Hours of work" does not include periods of rest during which the employee is not required to be available for work.

Rest Period: "Rest period" is any period which is not working time.

Public holiday: "Public holiday" is a day designated as such by the Second Schedule to the Organisation of Working Time Act 1997.

Lay-off: "Lay-off" means where an employee's employment ceases by reason of his employer's being unable to provide the work for which the employee was employed to do, and it is reasonable in the circumstances for that employer to believe that the cessation of employment will not be permanent, and the employer gives notice to that effect to the employee prior to the cessation.

Short Time: "Short-time" means where by reason of a diminution in the work provided for an employee by his employer, being work of a kind which, under his contract, the employee is employed to do, the employee's reduced hours of work for any week are less than one-half of his normal weekly hours.

Strike: A "strike" means the cessation of work by a body of persons employed, acting in combination; or a concerted refusal or a refusal under a common understanding of any number of persons employed, to continue to work for an employer in consequence of a dispute, done as a means of compelling their employer or any person or body of persons employed, or to aid other employees in compelling their employer or any person or body of persons employed, to accept or not to accept terms or conditions of or affecting employment. It may also include situations where the cessations of work are done as a means of compelling any person or body of persons employed, to accept or not to accept terms or conditions of, or affecting, employment.

Employees' Representatives: "Representatives of employees" means such trade unions as are, in the opinion of the appropriate Government Minister, representative of the employees in relation to whom the expression is used, or where there is no such trade union, such persons as are, in the opinion of the Minister, representative of such employees.

Employers' Representatives: "Representatives of employers" means such associations as are, in the opinion of the appropriate Government Minister, representative of the employers in relation to whom the expression is used, or where there is no such association, such persons as are, in the opinion of the Minister, representative of such employers.

Trade Union: "Trade union" means a body entitled under the Trade Union Act 1941 to carry on negotiations for the fixing of wages or other conditions of employment.

Tribunal: "The Tribunal" means the Employment Appeals Tribunal.

Red Circling: "Red Circling" means where for specific reasons an individual or group may not be required to perform what would normally be considered the full list of the duties of their grade and an arrangement is made whereby those concerned retain their grade while being reassigned to duties which, in the normal course, would attract a lower rate of pay. It also covers situations where the work of an employee or group of employees is of higher value to the company (see *Irish Crown Cork Co. v Desmond* ([1993] E.L.R. 180) and *Minister for Transport, Energy and Communications v Campbell* ([1996] E.L.R. 106)).

Comparator: A "comparator" is an employee in relation to the complainant or aggrieved employee, where both are employed by the same employer or associated employers and both employees concerned perform the same work ("like work") under the same or similar conditions or each is interchangeable with the other in relation to the work, or the work performed by one of the employees concerned is of the same or a similar nature to that performed by the other and any differences between the work performed or the conditions under which it is performed by each, either are of small importance in relation to the work as a whole or occur with such irregularity as not to be significant. Furthermore, the work performed by the complainant employee is equal or greater in value to the work performed by the other employee concerned, having regard to such matters as skill, physical or mental requirements, responsibility and working conditions but the aggrieved employee is paid less than the comparator, based on one of the discriminatory grounds. Where the comparator is a group, the group may contain employees who belong to the same category as the claimant employee. However, there is some doubt as to what the percentage or ratio should be—90 per cent without the discriminatory trait will be a valid comparator group; 50 per cent will not; and where the percentage is 75 per cent it is uncertain.

Like Work: "Like work" means where the actual work performed and the conditions under which it is performed are the same between the claimant and his/her comparator. In essence, it means the work performed by the claimant and comparator is of a broadly similar nature. However, jobs which are "radically different in content" may be compared.

Family Status: "Family status" means responsibility as a parent or as a person in *loco parentis* in relation to a person who has not attained the age of 18 years, or as a parent or the resident primary carer in relation to a person of or over that age with a disability, which is of such a nature as to give rise to the need for care or support on a continuing, regular or frequent basis. A primary carer is a resident primary carer in relation to a person with a disability if the primary carer resides with the person with the disability.

Marital Status: "Marital status" means single, married, separated, divorced or widowed.

Family Member: A "member of the family", in relation to any person, means that person's spouse, or a brother, sister, uncle, aunt, nephew, niece, lineal ancestor or lineal descendant of that person or that person's spouse.

Misconduct: No definition of "misconduct" is provided in the Act. In interpreting it, however, the EAT has taken a restrictive view of the types of misconduct which justify dismissal without notice or payment in lieu of notice: see *Lennon v Bredin* (M160/1978), holding that misconduct is "very bad behaviour of such a kind that no reasonable employer could be expected to tolerate the continuance of the relationship for a minute longer". See also *Creed v KMP Co-op Society Ltd UD* (187/1990 (reported at [1991] E.L.R. 140)). See, further, *Brewster v Burke* (High Court, February 8, 1978 (reported at (1985) 4 J.I.S.L.L.98)).

Remuneration: "Remuneration means not mere payment for work done but is what the doer expects to get as the result of the work he does in so far as what he expects to get is quantified in terms of money" (see *S &U Stores Ltd v Lee* ([1969] 2 All E.R. 417) approved in *McGivern v Irish National Insurance Co. Ltd* (P5/1982)). This definition covers all benefits based on the wage or salary received by the employee. In construing the similar definition in the equal pay legislation, the Labour Court has held that it is broad enough to include travel allowances, bonus payments, provision of a car, redundancy lump sum payment, hire purchase loans and sick pay.

Wages: "Wages" means any fee, bonus or commission, or any holiday, sick or maternity pay, or any other emolument referable to his employment, whether payable under his contract of employment or otherwise, and any sum payable to the employee upon the termination by the employer of his contract of employment without his having given to the employee the appropriate prior notice of the termination, being a sum paid in lieu of the giving of such notice. Wages do not include: any payment in respect of expenses incurred by the employee in carrying out his employment; any payment by way of a pension, allowance or gratuity in connection with the death, or the retirement or resignation from his employment, of the employee or as compensation for loss of office; any payment referable to the employee's redundancy; any payment to the employee otherwise than in his capacity as an employee; or any payment in kind or benefit in kind.

Pay: "Pay" means all amounts of payment, and any benefit in kind made or allowed by an employer to an employee in respect of the employee's employment.

Premium: "Premium" means any amount in excess of basic pay payable to an employee in respect of his or her work.

Cash: "Cash" means cash that is legal tender and includes both notes and coins.

Conditions of Employment: "Conditions of employment" includes conditions in respect of remuneration and matters related thereto (and, in relation to any pension scheme or arrangement, includes conditions for membership of the scheme or arrangement and entitlement to rights thereunder and conditions related to the making of contributions to the scheme or arrangement).

Local Authority: "Local authority" means a county council, a city council or a town council for the purposes of the Local Government Act 2001.

Sickness: "Sickness" or "illness" includes being incapable of work.

Social Insurance Fund: "The Social Insurance Fund" means the Social Insurance Fund established under s.39 of the Social Welfare Act 1952, and continued in being under s.122 of the Social Welfare (Consolidation) Act 1981 and further continued in being under s.7 of the Social Welfare (Consolidation) Act 1993.

Redundancy: "Redundancy" is where a dismissal is attributable wholly or mainly to the fact that an employer has ceased, or intends to cease, to carry on the business for the purposes of which the employee was employed, or has ceased or intends to cease, to carry on that business in the place where the employee was so employed, or the fact that the requirements of that business for employees to carry out work of a particular kind in the place where so employed has ceased or diminished or is expected to cease or diminish, or the fact that an employer has decided to carry on the business with fewer or no employees, whether by requiring the work for which the employee had been employed (or had been doing before the dismissal) to be done by other employees or otherwise, or the fact that an employer has decided that the work for which the employee had been employed (or had been doing before the dismissal) should henceforward be done in a different manner for which the employee is not sufficiently qualified or trained, or the fact that an employer has decided that the work for which the employee had been employed (or had been doing before the dismissal) should henceforward be done by a person who is also capable of doing other work for which the employee is not sufficiently qualified or trained.

(See *St Ledger v Frontline Distributors Ireland Ltd* ([1995] E.L.R. 160 at 161–162).

Dismissal: "Dismissal" means the termination by his employer of the employee's contract of employment with the employer, whether prior notice of the termination was or was not given to the employee, the termination by the employee of his contract of employment with his employer, whether prior notice of the termination was or was not given to the employer, in circumstances in which, because of the conduct of the employer, the employee was or would have been entitled, or it was or would have been reasonable for the employee, to terminate the contract of employment without giving prior notice of the termination to the employer (*constructive dismissal*), or the expiration of a contract of employment for a fixed term without its being renewed under the same contract or, in the case of a contract for a specified purpose (being a purpose of such a kind that the duration of the contract was limited but was, at the time of its making, incapable of precise ascertainment), the cesser of the purpose;

Resignation: "Resignation means a unilateral act which, if expressed in unambiguous and unconditional terms, brings a contract of employment to an end. The contract cannot be reconstructed by a subsequent unilateral withdrawal of the resignation. Where adequate notice is given, the contract is generally terminated in accordance with its terms and since there is no repudiation, the acceptance of the resignation by the employer is not required in order to determine the contract.

Company: "Company" means, except when the context otherwise requires, a company within the meaning of s.2 of the Companies Act 1963, or any other body corporate whether incorporated within or outside the State. Under the Companies Act 1963, it means "a company formed and registered under this Act, or an existing company".

Advertisement: "Advertisement" includes every form of advertisement, whether to the public or not and whether in a newspaper or other publication, on television or radio or by display of a notice or by any other means, and references to the publishing of advertisements shall be construed accordingly.

4. EQUALITY

The Employment Equality Act 1998, the Equal Status Act 2000 and the Equality Act 2004 deal with the issue of equality in employment. Employment equality in general terms means the right not to be discriminated against by virtue of a certain personal categorisation. The Act of 1998 is the main Act but it has been amended somewhat by the Act of 2000 and by the Act of 2004. Other statutes which impact on equality in employment are the Maternity Protection Acts 1994 and 2000 which address the issue of equal rights for pregnant employees both before and in the aftermath of pregnancy and the Protection of Employees (Part-Time Work) Act 2001 and Protection of Employees (Fixed-term Work) 2003, which provide that part-time and fixed-term contract workers should not be discriminated against solely on the basis of their part-time or fixed-term contract status (on these latter three Acts, see Chapters on Family Life and Legislation).

THE ACT OF 1998

The Employment Equality Act 1998, which came into operation on October 18, 1999, repealed the Anti-Discrimination (Pay) Act 1974 and the Employment Equality Act 1977. The Act outlaws discrimination on nine distinct grounds: gender, marital status, family status, sexual orientation, religion, age, disability, race and membership of the Traveller community. Harassment and sexual harassment, if related to any of the nine grounds, are deemed to be discrimination. Because the Act has undergone a referral under Art.26 of the Constitution, it is immune to constitutional challenge (see *In Re Article 26 and the Employment Equality Bill 1996* ([1997] 2 I.R. 321)). The Act deals with discrimination in work-related activities such as access to employment, pay and conditions of employment and vocational training. The Act applies in the main to employees of at least 18 years of age and under 65 years. However, the Act can also apply to persons under 18 years in vocational training (Section 12 and see *Byrne v An Foras Áiseanna Saothair* (DEC-E-2002/045)). The Act applies to all employers, associate employers and includes employment agencies. Further, an employer may be liable for the acts of employees done in the course of employment, whether the acts are done with the employer's knowledge or consent or not. The absence of such a provision was a major lacuna in the 1977 Act (see *A Health Board v BC* ([1994] E.L.R. 27)). An employer, however, can avoid liability by proving that he or she took reasonable steps to prevent the particular act of discrimination or that type of act generally.

Discrimination may be direct or indirect. Direct discrimination for the purpose of this Act occurs where one person is treated less favourably than another is, has been or would be treated in a comparable situation on any of the nine grounds set out in the Act; indirect discrimination occurs where an apparently neutral provision, criterion or practice would put persons belonging to any of the nine categories at a particular disadvantage compared with other persons, unless that provision, criterion or practice is objectively justified by a legitimate aim and the means of achieving that aim are appropriate and necessary (see, for example, *St. James's Hospital v Eng* (EDA3/2002), *Nuala Weir v St. Patrick's Hospital* ([2001] E.L.R. 228), *Bailey Gibson Ltd v Mathan* ([1998] E.L.R. 51) and *Janice Thompson v Tesco Ireland and Minister for Justice, Enterprise, Trade and Employment* ([2003] 14 E.L.R. 21).

Harassment is prohibited conduct and it shall be deemed to be discrimination within the meaning of the Act when it relates to any of the nine grounds and takes place with the purpose or effect of violating the dignity of a person and of creating an intimidating, hostile, degrading, humiliating or offensive environment. Where the harassment is based on the gender ground, it is deemed to be sexual harassment.

Victimisation is also prohibited and the Act provides that victimisation occurs where the dismissal or other penalisation of the complainant was solely, or mainly, occasioned by the complainant having, in good faith sought or intended to seek redress under this Act. The part-time and fixed-term contract Acts include a similar provision.

The Act has been amended somewhat by the Equal Status Act 2000 and by the Equality Act 2004.

The Act is divided into seven parts.

Part I deals with preliminary and general issues such as commencement, interpretation and definitions.

Part II deals with general provisions in relation to discrimination. It contains provisions regarding discrimination in specific areas. All the provisions in this part are applicable to all the discriminatory grounds.

Part III deals with specific provisions in relation to gender equality as between men and women. It introduces basic principles of equality which will be implied terms in every contract of employment (ss.18–27). Sections 19 and 20 deal with gender-based equal pay issues. The remaining sections deal with indirect discrimination. Section 23 deals specifically with sexual harassment in the workplace. This Part also contains provisions dealing with discriminatory action whose purpose is to foster equal opportunity between men and women. It deals with certain exceptions such as where the person's gender is a necessary occupational qualification. It is not prohibited discrimination for the purposes of the Act to confine a post to a man or a woman where gender is a bona fide occupational qualification by reason of the nature or the context in which the job is carried out (see *Brady v Irish TV Rentals Ltd* (DEE8/1985)). See also *Equality Officer in Parents Alone Resource Centre v Fozzard* (EE2/1988), where it was held that occupations providing individuals with personal services promoting their welfare were excluded employments for the purpose of the earlier equality statutes and see *Employment Equality Agency v Galway Social Service Council* (EE13/1983), where it was held that the gender of staff was not an occupational requirement for staff at a hostel for homeless men.

Part IV is a mirror image of Part III but applies to non-gender categories. It also deals with equal pay, indirect discrimination and non-sexual harassment.

Part V deals with the setting up of the Equality Authority, the statutory body for the development and progression of equality policy, its composition, its purposes, its functions and its powers.

Part VI deals with Equality reviews, action plans and reviewing the legislation.

Part VII deals with remedies and enforcement and related matters such as collective agreements, enforcement of decisions and the right to seek information. It also specifies certain criminal offences and outlines multiple remedies and alternative avenues for redress.

DISCRIMINATION

The Act is, in the main, concerned with discrimination against the nine categories of employees. However, positive discrimination for certain categories of employees is permitted and should be encouraged. This is referred to as permissible discrimination. Discrimination shall be taken to occur where, on any of the nine discriminatory grounds, one person is treated less favourably than another is, has been or would be treated. The less favourable treatment will usually manifest itself in unequal pay, access to promotion, training, conditions of employment, classification of employment, promotion and by harassment. There is no requirement that the act in question be done with an intention to discriminate. These provisions are what have been described as "result directed rather than intention directed" (see *St. James's Hospital v Eng* (EDA3/2002)). The duty not to discriminate has also been described as one of strict liability, not subject to a requirement of fault (see *Southern Health Board v Mitchell* (DEE2/1999 reported at [1999] E.L.R. 322)).

The nine prohibited discriminatory grounds set out in s.6 as between two persons are:

(a) that one is a woman and the other is a man—"the gender ground";

(b) that they are of different marital status—"the marital status ground";

(c) that one has family status and the other does not—"the family status ground";

(d) that they are of different sexual orientation—"the sexual orientation ground";

(e) that one has a different religious belief from the other, or that one has a religious belief and the other has not—"the religion ground";

(f) that they are of different ages, being between 18 years and 65 years in that one is older than the other—as "the age ground";

(g) that one is a person with a disability and the other either is not or is a person with a different disability—"the disability ground";

(h) that they are of different race, colour, nationality or ethnic or national origin—"the ground of race";

(i) that one is a member of the Traveller community and the other is not—"the Traveller community ground".

The grounds are referred to as "gender" and "non-gender grounds", item (a) above being the gender ground and the remaining items (b) to (i) being the non-gender ground.

In addition to setting out nine discriminatory grounds, s.8 of the Act also sets out specific areas where discriminatory treatment should not occur against an employee, prospective employee or agency worker. These specific areas are:

(a) access to employment;

(b) conditions of employment;

(c) training or experience for or in relation to employment;

(d)   promotion or re-grading; or
(e)   classification of posts.

An employer or provider of agency workers is under an obligation not to have in place rules or instructions, or otherwise apply or operate a practice which would result in discrimination against an employee or class of employees in relation to conditions of employment.

As stated above, the specific areas targeted by the Act where discrimination should not, in particular, occur are access to employment, conditions of employment, training or experience for or in relation to employment, promotion or re-grading, or classification of posts. The categories where discrimination should not occur are not exhaustive.

Access to employment and conditions of employment are two areas that have generated a significant amount of activity.

Access to employment will encompass such matters as how advertising and interviews are conducted. Because advertising and interviewing are included, the Act affords protection even to prospective employees.

As regards advertising, s.10 provides that it is unlawful to advertise a job in such a way that the advertisement could reasonably be interpreted as indicating an intention to discriminate. See, for example, *Employment Equality Agency v Cork Examiner Publications Ltd* (EE13/1990); *Employment Equality Agency v Group 4 Securitas Ireland Ltd* (DEE1/1993), where the advertisement indicated that the job "may be of particular interest to married women". There is no provision for an individual complainant to refer a claim of discriminatory advertising. Section 85 provides that such claims may be referred by the Equality Authority and in *Burke v FAS* (DEC-E2004-016), an Equality Officer said that it was clear that the intention of the legislature was to give the Authority the sole power to institute proceedings against discriminatory advertisements. The first case to be decided under s.10 was *The Equality Authority v Ryanair* ([2001] E.L.R. 107), where the Authority complained of an advertisement which stipulated that the company needed "a young and dynamic professional". The Equality Officer found that the use of the word "young" indicated, or might reasonably be understood as indicating, an intention to exclude applicants who were "not young" and that the use of the word "young" as a requirement in the advertisement constituted discrimination on the age ground. Both the advertiser and the publisher may be found guilty of the offence.

Where a competitive interview method of selection has been adopted, the many cases under the 1977 Act stress that it is not a question of determining who was the most meritorious candidate, but whether the gender or any other non-gender characteristics of the complainant influenced the choice of the interview or selection board. Account will be taken as to whether the interview was conducted in a non-discriminatory manner. Were discriminatory questions asked? See *Medical Council v Barrington* (EE9/1988), where a single female alleged that she was asked whether she was thinking of getting married, a question not asked of the male and married female interviewees. In *Good v City of Cork V.E.C.* (EE29/1997), it was held that where a successful candidate is selected on the basis of performance at interview, what had to be considered was not just whether the interview was conducted in a non-discriminatory manner, but also whether there were "credible and non-discriminatory reasons for not selecting the candidate". In *McDonald v Clonmel Healthcare Ltd* (DEC-E2001-012), the Equality Officer held that the employer discriminated against the claimant by discussing matters relative to her marital and family circumstances during the course of the interview process. In *Phelan v Michael Stein Travel* ([1999] E.L.R. 58), a note was taken that the particular claimant interviewee was married with two children. No similar note was taken in relation to any other candidate. It was deemed to be discrimination on the family status ground. See also *Trinity College Dublin v McGhee* (EE1/1989) and *Corrib Airport Ltd v A Worker* (DEE3/1989).

Gender-Based Discrimination

Part III sets out specific provisions relating to equality between women and men, the "gender ground". The provisions in this Part regarding the definition of sexual harassment have been replaced by s.8 of the Equality Act 2004. (Section 21 of the Act inserts a gender equality clause into any contract which does not contain one. However, a gender equality clause shall not operate in relation to a difference between a woman's contract of employment and a man's contract of employment if the employer proves that the difference is genuinely based on grounds other than the gender ground).

Gender discrimination may be direct or indirect. Indirect discrimination occurs when "a measure distinguishing between employees ... has in practice an adverse impact on substantially more members of one or other sex ... unless the employer establishes that it is based on objectively justified factors unrelated to any discrimination on grounds of sex" (see Case C–127/92 *Enderby v Frenchay Health Authority* ([1993] E.C.R. I-5535). See also *Bailey Gibson Ltd v Mathan* ([1998] E.L.R. 51), where the Supreme Court held that if it is shown that a practice complained of "bore significantly more heavily on members of the claimant's sex than on members of the other sex, the claimant had established a prima facie case of discrimination and the onus of proof then shifted to the respondent to show that the practice in question was based on objectively verifiable factors which had no relation to the claimant's sex". In *Nuala Weir v St Patrick's Hospital* ([2001] E.L.R. 228), the Equality Officer concluded that the respondent indirectly discriminated against the claimant by having in place a policy whereby supervisory-level staff could not job-share because this said policy adversely affected more females than males. The applicant in *Janice Thompson v Tesco Ireland and Minister for Justice, Enterprise, Trade and Employment* ([2003] 14 E.L.R. 21), however, was not successful in establishing that the practice of working late bore significantly more heavily on single mothers because they needed to avail of child-minding than on single men. Collective agreements which disadvantaged part-time workers, most of whom were female, is indirect discrimination (see *IMPACT v Irish Aviation Authority* ([2000] E.L.R. 29)).

As regards the necessary statistical evidence and the test for "objective justification", see *Inoue v NBK Designs Ltd* ([2003] E.L.R. 98). In this case, the Labour Court was satisfied that the dismissal of a part-time secretary following the employer's decision to amalgamate two part-time positions into a single full-time post was indirect discrimination on the gender ground and the family and marital status grounds, in circumstances where this part-time secretary, who had job-shared, was a female lone-parent with a school-going child.

In gender discrimination claims, the claimant must establish, on the balance of probabilities, facts from which it may be presumed that the claimant has suffered discrimination. In *Fiona O'Hanlon v Educational Building Society* ([2002] 13 E.L.R. 107), it was held that it is "only when this burden is discharged by the claimant that a *prima facie* case of discrimination has been raised and the onus shifts to the respondent to prove that there was no infringement" of the Employment Act 1998.

Of particular importance in the gender area is the principle of equal pay for equal work and there is implied into all contracts a term entitling the worker to such equal pay. Thus, men and women are entitled to the same rate of remuneration for like work (be it under a contract of employment or employment under a contract to personally execute any work or labour) with the same employer or with an associated employer. There must be, however, an actual concrete real life comparator of the other sex performing like work within the same establishment or service (see *Brides v Minister for Agriculture* [1998] 4 I.R. 250 at 270 and Case 43/75 *Defrenne v SABENA (No.2)* [1976] E.C.R. 455). This comparator need not be contemporaneously employed; they may be the claimant's predecessor or successor, although there is a time limit of three years either side of the claimant's employment. The provision will not be contravened if different rates of remuneration are paid to different employees on grounds other than the gender ground (see *C & D Food Ltd v Cunnion* ([1997] 1 I.R. 147 at 151). The onus of proof is on the employer to prove that the differentiation is genuinely attributable to grounds other than sex (see *Irish Crown Cork Co. v Desmond* ([1993] E.L.R. 180) and *Minister for Transport, Energy and Communications v Campbell* ([1996] E.L.R. 106). In these cases, "red circling" was put forward as the objective ground justifying any discriminatory treatment (see also *Printech International Ltd v Cotter* (DEP1/2000) and *Flynn v Primark (No.2)* [1999] E.L.R. 89). In *Roches Stores v MANDATE* (DEP3/2001), the Labour Court considered whether the "red circling" of the comparator's pay was "objectively justifiable" and the court accepted that it was.

Positive Gender Discrimination

The Act allows for positive action or measures to promote equal opportunities for men and women, in particular by removing existing inequalities which affect women's opportunities. See Case C–450/93 *Kalanke v Freie und Hansestadt Bremen* ([1995] E.C.R. I-3051), where the European Court of Justice while recognising that enactment of such measures, although discriminatory in appearance, were permissible if they were designed to eliminate or reduce actual instances of inequality but where the court held at the same time that it could not be understood as legitimising national rules which guaranteed women absolute and unconditional priority for appointment or promotion. In a later case, the Court of Justice modified its stance somewhat and ruled the legislation did not preclude a national rule under which a female candidate may be granted preference, provided that the candidates possess equivalent merits and the candidates are subjected to an objective assessment which takes account of the specific personal situation of all the candidates (see Case C–407/98 *Abrahamsson v Fogelqvist* [2000] E.C.R. I-5539).

An employer may arrange or provide special treatment to women "in connection with pregnancy or childbirth" without contravening the non-discriminatory provisions of the Act. This type of discrimination is considered positive discrimination and is lawful.

Non-Gender Discrimination

Non-gender discrimination will be discrimination based on grounds of age, disability, family/marital status, sexual orientation, race, religion or member of the Traveller community. Harassment, if related to any of these grounds, may constitute non-gender discrimination. The provision in the Act of 1998 defining harassment has been replaced by s.8 of the Equality Act 2004. There is inserted into every contract of employment, which does not already contain one, a non-discriminatory equality clause. Non-gender discrimination may be direct or indirect. Indirect discrimination occurs where a requirement, practice or otherwise relating to employment, though it applies to all the employees or prospective employees of a particular employer, operates to the disadvantage of one employee as compared with other employees in relation to any of the discriminatory grounds and cannot be justified as being reasonable in all the circumstances of the case.

Some of the areas that have generated a significant amount of case law are discrimination on the age ground, the disability ground and the family/marital status grounds.

Age Ground: In *A Firm of Solicitors v A Worker* ([2002] E.L.R. 305), the first age-related case, the Labour Court found that the worker's dismissal resulted from the employer's decision to employ a younger person and that there was thus discrimination on the age ground.

Disability Ground: For the purposes of the Act, a person with a disability is to be considered fully competent and capable to undertake the duties attached to a job, if the person could do the duties with the assistance of special treatment or facilities. This obligation is subject to the "nominal cost" requirement. The definition of "nominal" is not the same for every employer or enterprise (see *A Motor Company v A Worker* (DEE6/2002) and *Bowes v Southern Regional Fisheries Board* (DEC-E2004-008)). In *A Computer Component Company v A Worker* ([2002] E.L.R. 124), which was a disability-related dismissal case, an employee was dismissed because she suffered from epilepsy. The Labour Court held that there was discrimination on the disability ground.

Family/Marital Status Ground: Regarding the concept of "nominal cost" or the economic defence where an employer is confronted with a disability/incapacity situation, the employer is obliged to take appropriate measures to provide special facilities unless to do so would involve a disproportionate burden on the employer. The following are factors that can be taken into account when assessing whether a burden is disproportionate or not:

- The financial costs.
- The scale of the operation.
- The number of beneficiaries.
- The disruption that may be caused.
- The benefit to the employee in question.
- The possibility of public funding such as grants.
- Any benefit that might accrue to the employer.

Discrimination on the basis of family or marital status is prohibited. In *Eagle Star v A Worker* ([1998] E.L.R. 306), an employee was excluded from special benefits on the basis that he was cohabiting rather than married (see also *Phelan v Michael Stein Travel,* mentioned above).

Positive Non-Gender Discrimination

Positive discrimination is not only permitted but should be encouraged. Positive discrimination, or positive action as it is referred to in the Act, allows for special measures for persons over the age of 50, persons with a disability and members of the Traveller community. Positive discrimination is to facilitate the integration into employment of these categories of persons and to reduce or eliminate the effects of discrimination and to promote equal opportunities by removing existing inequalities (see *Abrahamsson v Fogelqvist* and *In Re Article 26 and the Employment Equality Bill 1996* ([1997] 2 I.R. 321)).

Section 35 allows for special rates of remuneration for employees with a disability (*i.e.* lower remuneration based on productivity) and for other special treatment or facilities.

Requirements as to residency, citizenship or proficiency in the Irish language that would normally be considered discrimination may be permitted for certain posts in the public sector. Discrimination on age or disability grounds is permitted in certain employments such as in the Defence Forces, in An Garda Síochána, or in the prison service (see *In Re Article 26 and the Employment Equality Bill 1996*). However, this provision has been amended by the Act of 2004 and there is now a requirement to show that the occupational qualification is legitimately objective and that the requirement is proportionate.

The Comparator

Discrimination occurs where one employee is treated differently as compared to another employee, to his/her detriment, and when the discriminatory treatment is related to any one of the nine grounds set out in the Act, it is actionable discrimination for the purposes of the Act. The employee with whom the claimant employee compares himself/herself is called the "comparator". So what is a comparator? For the purpose of the Act, s.28 provides that where two persons who differ as regards one or more of the nine grounds, employed by the same employer or an associate employer and doing like work, one is a comparator of the other. The definition does not encompass the concept of a "hypothetical comparator". A claimant must be able to point to "an actual concrete real life comparator" performing like work (see *Brides v Minister for Agriculture* ([1998] 4 I.R. 250 at 270)). The definition in the part-time workers and fixed-term contract workers Acts is significantly wider than that provided for in the 1998 Act in so far as a fixed-term contract worker and a part-time worker are permitted to compare themselves to another worker engaged in the same industry or sector but employed by a different employer; whereas the 1998 Act restricts the comparison to workers within the same or associated companies. However, part-time workers and fixed-term contract workers' wider net of comparators is only permissible in circumstances where no comparator is available in the employment of the employer or associate employer.

Like Work

There must be like work between the claimant and the chosen comparator. "Like work" is where the actual work performed and the conditions under which it is performed are the same between the claimant and his/her comparator. The Act defines like work as: work where the claimant and the comparator both perform the same work under the same or similar conditions; or each is interchangeable with the other in relation to the work—the work performed by one is of a similar nature to that performed by the other and any differences between the work performed or the conditions under which it is performed by each either are of small importance in relation to the work as a whole or occur with such irregularity as not to be significant to the work as a whole; or the work performed by one is equal in value to the work performed by the other, having regard to such matters as skill, physical or mental requirements, responsibility and working conditions. In *Toyota Motor Distributors (Ireland) Ltd v Kavanagh* (EP17/1985, DEP1/1986), it was held whether differences between two jobs are of small importance depends on how sufficiently important those differences are to justify payment of a higher rate in respect of one of the jobs concerned (see also *Murphy v Bord Telecom Eireann* ([1988] E.C.R. 673) and the subsequent decision of Keane J., reported at ([1989] I.L.R.M. 53)). For an excellent example of the methodology employed in assessing a work of equal value claim, see *Sweeney v Labour Relations Commission* (EP10/1997).

In relation to the work which an agency worker is employed to do, no person except another agency worker may be regarded as employed to do like work (and, accordingly, in relation to the work which a non-agency worker is employed to do, an agency worker may not be regarded as employed to do like work).

Redress

The forum for seeking redress at first instance in all cases, except cases involving dismissal which go to the Labour Court, is to the Director of Equality Investigations. A claim for redress for discrimination on grounds of gender *may* be brought to the Circuit Court instead of the Director or the Labour Court. In these circumstances the Circuit Court has unlimited jurisdiction whereas the Labour Court is limited to the maximum under s.82 of the Act. In a case of discrimination or victimisation, a claim for redress must be initiated within six months of the most recent occurrence of the alleged act of discrimination or victimisation (see *A Named Female Employee v A Named Respondent* (DEC-E2003-001)). In exceptional circumstance, this six-month period may be extended to 12 months. (See *Gowran & District Community Employment Scheme v A Worker* (EET1/2002). See also *Tyco Healthcare (Ireland) Ltd v A Worker* (EET5/2002)). In *Fitzsimons-Markey v Gaelscoil Thulach na nOg* ([2004] E.L.R. 110), the Labour Court said that the question of whether an applicant had been prevented by "exceptional circumstances" was "pre-eminently a question of fact and degree" and not only must an applicant show the existence of "exceptional circumstances" but also that those circumstances operated to prevent the applicant from lodging the claim in time.

There is a right of appeal to the Labour Court against a decision of the Director and, in determining an appeal, the Labour Court may provide for any form of redress which the Director could have ordered.

A dismissal case (heard in the first instance by the Labour Court), may appeal to the Circuit Court. The Labour Court may refer a point of law to the High Court.

A claimant may bring a simultaneous referral of a complaint of discriminatory treatment to the Director and a complaint of discriminatory dismissal to the Labour Court (see, for instance, *O'Hanlon v Educational Building Society* ([2002] E.L.R. 107)).

A claim involving discrimination in recruitment by the Civil Service or Local Appointments Commission, the Garda Síochána or the Defence Forces must first be referred to the recruitment authority concerned.

The Office of the Director of Equality Investigations has no jurisdiction to investigate the substance of the allegations by complainants employed in an Embassy by virtue of the Embassy's claim of sovereign immunity (see *O'Shea v Italian Embassy* [2002] E.L.R. 276). This is in line with the decision of the Supreme Court in *Government of Canada v Employment Appeals Tribunal* ([1992] I.L.R.M. 325).

Nor do the Labour Court and/or the ODEI have jurisdiction to hear a claim unless the claimant habitually carries out his or her work in the State (see *A Retail Company v A Worker* ([2001] E.L.R. 358) and *A Complainant v A Company* ([2003] E.L.R. 333)).

There is also a facility for mediation in the Act. The Director of Equality Investigations may refer a case for mediation where it appears to the Director that the case could be resolved in that way. Similarly, the Labour Court may attempt to resolve a case by mediation or refer it to the Director for mediation. A case will not be referred for mediation if there is an objection from either party (see *A Male Complainant v A Bar and Restaurant* (DEC-E2003-005)).

Redress, which may be ordered by the ODEI or the Labour Court, is as follows:

(1) in an equal pay case, equal pay and arrears in respect of a period not exceeding three years before the date of referral;

(2) equal treatment and compensation of up to a maximum of two years' pay, or the sum specified in the Act where the person is not an employee;

(3) in a dismissal case, reinstatement or re-engagement with or without compensation subject to a maximum of two years' pay.

Compensation in lieu of re-instatement or re-engagement may be ordered against an employer who has failed to comply with an order of reinstatement or re-engagement made by the Labour Court, up to a maximum of two years' pay. In measuring the appropriate quantum of compensation, regard must be had to all the effects which flowed from the discrimination. These include "not only the financial loss suffered by the complainant arising from the discrimination but also the distress and indignity ... suffered in consequence thereof, including the effects of bringing ... proceedings" (see *Fox v Lee* (DEE6/2003) and *McGinn v Daughters of Charity* (EDA9/2003)). In gender equality cases, the Director or the court may award interest on any compensation awarded. The Director or the court may also order any person to take "a specified course of action". Where a gender equality case is initiated in the Circuit Court, that court may order any of the forms of redress set out.

The Equality Authority, or a person affected, may refer a collective agreement to the Director of Equality Investigations where it is considered that any provision of the agreement is discriminatory (see *Noonan Services Ltd v Labour Court*, unreported, High Court, February 25, 2004).

5. FAMILY LIFE AND EMPLOYMENT LAW

An employee may become the recipient of a bundle of statutory rights by virtue of some facet of his/her family life status. Various statutes have been enacted with a view to reconciling occupational and family obligations. For example, a pregnant employee has rights under the Maternity Protection Act 1994 (as amended), a prospective adopting parent has rights under the Adoptive Leave Act 1995, the Carer's Leave Act 2001 provides for the temporary absence from employment of employees for the purpose of the provision of full-time care and attention to a person requiring it and the Parental Leave Act 1998 and the Parental Leave (Amendment) Act 2005 provides for an entitlement for men and women to avail of unpaid parental leave to enable them to take care of their young children. This Act also contains provision for limited paid leave for employees in family crises — to be known as *force majeure* leave. The Employment Equality Act confers entitlements on an employee not to be discriminated against by virtue of his "family status" or "marital status" (on Employment Equality, see Chapter 4.)

THE MATERNITY PROTECTION ACT 1994, AS AMENDED BY THE MATERNITY PROTECTION (AMENDMENT) ACT 2004

The purpose of the Act, which came into operation on January 30, 1995 and which implements Council Directive 92/85/EEC, is to protect a woman's biological condition during and after pregnancy (see Case C–411/96 *Boyle v Equal Opportunities Commission* [1998] E.C.R. 1-6401). The Act re-enacts with amendments the provisions of the Maternity Protection of Employees Act 1981. The key right guaranteed in the Act is the right not to be dismissed because of the pregnancy.

Under the Act there is a right to maternity leave with continuity of service preserved and the right to return to the same job or a job no less favourable. There are provisions in the Act for extension of the leave and for additional leave and there is a right to time off for ante-natal and post-natal care. Importantly, there is a right to equal pay for pregnant employees. A male employee is entitled to leave where the mother of his new child dies.

The Act of 2004 provides for a reduction in the compulsory pre-confinement period of maternity leave from four weeks to two weeks and it allows expectant mothers to attend ante-natal classes without loss of pay. The Act of 2004 also gives a right to fathers to paid time off to attend two ante-natal classes. Other rights in this Act are adjustment of working hours or breaks for breastfeeding mothers, termination of additional maternity leave in the event of illness—subject to the agreement of the employer, and absence from work on additional maternity leave to count for employment rights such as seniority and annual leave.

Maternity Leave

The right to maternity leave is probably the most significant right in the Act and the one that is availed of by all pregnant employees. This leave known as "maternity leave", is for a minimum period of not less than 18 consecutive weeks, allocated in a continuous period of at least 14 weeks before and/or after confinement. There are certain conditions precedent to the taking of leave and returning to work, in particular, there is a notification requirement. The EAT consistently took the view that the statutory entitlement to take maternity leave, conferred by the very similarly worded s.9 of the 1981 Act, was dependent on strict compliance with its provisions and that failure to comply could not be excused by reason of the employee's ignorance of the statutory requirements (see, for example, *O'Flaherty v Coughlan* (P8/1983)). However, where the employee has failed to notify the employer, she may still have a contractual right to maternity leave and as a consequence a right to return to work (see *Scott v Yeates & Sons Opticians Ltd* ([1992] E.L.R. 83)). Alternatively, the employer may be estopped by its conduct from raising the question of non-compliance (see, for example, *Butler v Smurfit Ireland Ltd* (P3/1988) and *Morgan v Dunnes Stores (Cork) Ltd* (UD 761/1987)). In addition to the minimum 18 week period of maternity leave, pregnant employees are entitled to an optional eight weeks' additional leave.

Entitlement to return to work is conditional on compliance with the notification requirements set out in s.28 of the Act. Since resumption in the same job might not be practicable in every case, s.27 allows for the provision of suitable alternative work. See *Tighe v Travenol Laboratories (Ireland) Ltd* ([1989] 8 J.I.S.L.L. 124) where the EAT said that the word "suitable" means "suitable in relation to the employee concerned". The words should be interpreted "subjectively from the employee's standpoint, including the general nature of the work which suited her and her domestic considerations" (see also *Butler v Smurfit Ireland Ltd* (P3/1988), *Savino v Gardner Merchant (Ireland) Ltd* (P7/ 1990) and *McCormack v Brady* (P30/1992)). In *Yvonne Maguire v*

Aer Lingus ([2001] E.L.R. 355), the claimant returned to work and was informed that her previous job no longer existed due to downsizing of the respondent. Her alternative duties were outlined but there was a lack of clarity as to the nature of the work she would be expected to do. The Rights Commissioner made an award of compensation and noted that the uncertainty surrounding the future of the claimant's conditions of employment did not meet the requirements of the Act regarding suitable alternative work and that the employer had exploited the claimant's absence on maternity leave and attempted to exploit her vulnerability when she returned. This case shows the strength of the level of protection under this Act.

Equal Pay

It is a matter for the employment contract as to what amount (if anything) women are paid by their employer, when they take maternity leave. The important issue is that they are permitted, without suffering any prejudice, other than loss of remuneration, to take the statutory minimum term of leave. It is on the Member State that the obligation to provide entitlement to pay lies rather than on the employer (see Case 184/83 *Hofmann v Barmer Ersatzkasse* [1984] E.C.R. 3047 and Case C–342/93 *Gillespie v Northern Health and Social Services Board* [1996] E.C.R. 475). Note that the Pregnant Workers Directive (Directive 92/85/EEC ([1992] O.J. L348/1) provides that payment to workers on maternity leave must be an "adequate" allowance.

The right of a pregnant employee to equal pay means that pregnancy and confinement are not in themselves reasons for reducing an employee's remuneration. However, an employer is not necessarily required to pay full salary to employees absent from work on maternity leave. See Case C–342/93 *Gillespie v Northern Health and Social Services Board* ([1996] E.C.R. 475), where the plaintiffs who were off work on maternity leave were entitled to be paid for such leave but were not to be paid their full salary but rather a reduced salary for the period of their maternity leave. The European Court of Justice held that the "equal pay" principle had not been contravened and that how much women in those circumstances should be paid, either directly by their employer or else through the social security system, was a matter for the Member States provided that the amount was not so low as to deter women from availing of their minimum maternity leave.

In *Gillespie,* the European Court of Justice also ruled that a woman on maternity leave must receive a pay rise awarded before or during maternity leave. The principle of non-discrimination required that a woman who was still employed during maternity leave must, like any other worker, benefit from any pay rise. The court said that to deny such an increase to a woman on maternity leave would discriminate against her since, had she not been pregnant, she would have received the pay rise.

The EAT has ruled that employees are entitled to be paid for the public holidays which fall during maternity leave (see *Forde v Des Gibney Ltd* (P8/1985)).

Right not to be dismissed

An employer is precluded from dismissing a pregnant employer on the basis of her pregnancy. In Case C–394/96 *Brown v Rentokil Ltd* ([1998] E.C.R. I-4185), the European Court of Justice ruled that the Equal Treatment Directive precluded dismissal of a female worker at any time during her pregnancy for absences due to incapacity for work caused by illness resulting from that pregnancy. Importantly, the one year service requirement does not apply to employees dismissed for pregnancy, giving birth or breastfeeding or any matters connected therewith. The dismissal of a pregnant woman recruited for an indefinite period cannot be justified on grounds relating to her inability, on a temporary basis, to fulfil a fundamental condition of her employment contract, namely to perform the work for which she had been engaged. Protection afforded to a woman during pregnancy cannot be dependent on whether her presence at work during maternity was essential to the proper functioning of the undertaking in which she was employed. Further, an employer is precluded from dismissing a female worker on the ground of pregnancy, notwithstanding that she was recruited for a fixed period, failed to inform the employer that she was pregnant even though she was aware of this when the contract of employment was entered into and, because of her pregnancy, was unable to work during a substantial part of the term of that contract. The principle of equal treatment also precludes dismissal of a female worker at any time during her pregnancy for absence due to incapacity for work caused by illness resulting from the pregnancy. The Labour Court has summarised the position as being that "no employee can be dismissed while they are pregnant unless there are exceptional circumstances unconnected with the pregnancy and those exceptional circumstances are notified to the employee in writing" (see, for example, *Carroll v Cullen* (DEE13/2002)). For an example of a case in which an employer succeeded in justifying a dismissal during pregnancy, see *Mason v Winston's Jewellers* ([2003] E.L.R. 108).

The issue as to the onus of proof in alleged pregnancy-related dismissals was fully considered in *Pedreschi v Burke* (UD 591/1999), where the claimant submitted that the onus of proof remained on the employer. This was rejected by the EAT which held that, in such a case, the claimant bore the onus of proof.

Redress

Disputes go to the Rights Commissioner at first instance within a period of six months from the date on which the employer is informed of the initial circumstances relevant to the dispute. The Rights Commissioner may extend the period as is reasonable but not exceeding 12 months. An appeal lies to the EAT within four weeks of the date on which the decision is given. There is a further appeal to the High Court on a point of law. Additionally, the EAT may refer a question of law arising in proceedings before it to the High Court for determination by it.

Redress may consist of the following:

(a) the grant of leave for such period as may be so specified;
(b) an award for compensation in favour of the employee to be paid by the relevant employer.

Compensation shall be of such amount as is just and equitable having regard to all the circumstances of the case but shall not exceed 20 weeks' remuneration.

Where an employee has been dismissed due to pregnancy or matters related, redress for unfair dismissal should be taken under the Unfair Dismissals Acts (see *Webb v EMO Air Cargo (UK) Ltd (No.2)* ([1996] 1 W.L.R. 1454)). See also *Lee v Fox* (EED 0361), a case that involved a dismissal allegedly on the basis of pregnancy. The claimant announced that she was pregnant and shortly afterwards was dismissed for misconduct. In *Lee,* it was held that in awarding compensation for a discriminatory dismissal the Labour Court is not restricted to the financial loss suffered by the claimant but can award compensation for the "distress and indignity" suffered as well.

The Adoptive Leave Acts 1995 and 2005

These Acts, which came into operation on March 1995 and January 2005, set out the framework for leave for adopting parents. Section 3 of the 2005 Act provides for a minimum period of leave of 16 consecutive weeks commencing on the date of placement for adopting mothers and sole male adopters and for other adopting fathers in certain very limited circumstances such as where the adopting mother of the child dies (see s.6, 2005 Act). In certain circumstances this leave may, on request, be postponed such as when an adoptive child is in hospital (see s.9, 2005 Act). There is provision for a further additional period of up to eight consecutive weeks' additional adoptive leave, immediately following the 16 weeks' adoptive leave period (see s.4, 2005 Act). Entitlement to such additional leave is conditional on the employer being informed in writing not later than four weeks before the expected date of return from adoptive leave. In the case of a foreign adoption, subject to certain notification requirements, some or all of the period of additional leave may be taken before the day of placement. In addition to adoptive leave, there is an entitlement to time off from work, without loss of pay, to attend any pre-adoption classes and meetings which the employee is obliged to attend (see s.7, 2005 Act). Pay in respect of the 16 week period is covered by a social welfare payment but the optional eight weeks' additional leave is leave without pay from either the employer or from the State.

The obligations or entitlements under these Acts cannot be contracted out of. Provision of arrangements that are more favourable than those provided in the Acts are permissible.

In Case 162/83 *Commission v Italy* ([1983] E.C.R. 3273), the European Court of Justice held that the restriction of adoptive leave, under Italian legislation, to women, was justified by the State's legitimate concern to assimilate as far as possible the condition of entry of the child into the adopting family. The difference in treatment between adopting mothers and fathers could not, therefore, be regarded as discrimination. In *Telecom Éireann v O'Grady* ([1998] 3 I.R. 432), where the adopting father's application for adoptive leave was refused by Telecom Éireann on the basis that such leave was available for female employees only, the High Court said that as a result of the decisions of the European Court of Justice in cases such as *Commission v Italy*, a Member State could legitimately restrict the availability of adoptive leave to female employees. He noted, however, that the Oireachtas, in enacting s.16, could have chosen to permit an employer to arrange for or provide special treatment to women in connection with "pregnancy and maternity" or "pregnancy and motherhood" but it chose to restrict the concession or exemption to "pregnancy and childbirth" and thus did not include the provision of special treatment to adopting mothers. The decision was upheld on appeal by the Supreme Court ([1998] 3 I.R. 432, 447) who held that the provisions of s.16 of the 1977 Act were "quite clear and explicit and no matter what manner of interpretation is applied thereto are incapable of being interpreted as to include adoption". In their view the scheme which allowed for adoptive leave for adopting females was "clearly discriminatory against male persons". Consequently, any voluntary or contractual scheme for adoptive leave cannot be confined to female employees (see also *Merriman v Eastern Health Board* (EE10/1998) and *Doolan v Dublin Institute of Technology* (DEE 8/1998)). The arrangements for civil servants are now set out in Department of Finance Circular 2/97, clause 4 of which provides that civil servants on adoptive leave will be given full pay, except where he or she has been appointed for a fixed term of less than 26 weeks. Moreover, clause 10 provides that adoptive leave for fathers is only available if the adopting mother dies within a specified time of the day of placement.

Absence from work on adoptive leave shall not affect any right of the employee related to employment (other than the right to remuneration during the absence). In effect, the employee absent on adoptive leave is deemed to have been in the employment of the employer. There is a general right to return to work on expiry of adoptive leave or additional adoptive leave. Entitlement to return to work is conditional on compliance with the notification requirements. Because resumption in the same job might not be practicable in every case, provision is made in the legislation for suitable alternative work. The words "suitable in relation to the employee concerned" will be construed subjectively from the employee's standpoint (see *Tighe v Travenol Laboratories Ltd* (P14/1986) — a decision under the Maternity Protection of Employees Act 1981, reported at (1989) 8 J.I.S.L.L. 124)).

Redress

Redress is sought at first instance from a Rights Commissioner not later than six months from the day of placement, or where there is no placement, within six months from the date on which the employer is notified of the intention to take adoptive leave. The six month period may be extended for a further six months where the Rights

Commissioner considers it reasonable to so do. An appeal lies to the EAT. There is a further appeal on a point of law to the High Court (see s.36). Redress may consist of an award of compensation of such amount as is just and equitable having regard to all the circumstances but not exceeding 20 weeks' remuneration in favour of the adopting parent, to be paid by the relevant employer and/or a direction to the employer to comply with the legislation.

The Parental Leave Act 1998 and the Parental Leave (Amendment) Act 2005

The main Act, which came into operation on December 3, 1998, provides for an entitlement for men and women employees who have completed one year's continuous employment to avail of unpaid parental leave for a period of up to 14 weeks to enable them to take care of their young children, whether these children are natural or adoptive children. Under the Act of 1995, the leave is not transferable between parents. However, this is amended by the Act of 2005 to allow that parental leave is transferable between parents where both parents are employed by the same employer. Though not specifically stated in the Act, such transfer of leave between parents may be subject to the agreement of the employer. Under the Act of 1995, where two children are born close together there is 14 weeks per child but no more than 14 weeks in any 12 month period unless there is agreement to that effect. There is nothing that precludes an employer from putting in place arrangements which are more favourable to the employee but the provisions of the Act cannot be contracted out of (see s.4). Whilst the leave is unpaid leave it is counted as reckonable service. The employer may pay for the leave but is not required to do so under the Act. The full entitlement can only be taken following a year's continuous employment but there are reduced entitlements for employees with more than three months' continuous employment of one week parental leave per month of service.

The Act also contains provision for limited paid leave for employees in family crises to be known as *force majeure* leave.

The key features of the Act, as amended, are that the parents or persons acting in *loco parentis* of children born or adopted on or after December 3, 1993 are entitled to:

(i)   a total of 14 weeks' leave for such a child;
(ii) the leave must be taken before a child is five; (The Act

of 2005 has amended the age of the child from five to under eight years of age and if a child has a disability to under 16 years of age. In the case of an adopted child who has on or before the date of the adoption order attained the age of six years of age but is under eight years of age an employee may avail of parental leave not later than two years from the date of the adoption order).

(iii) the leave may be taken as a continuous block or, by agreement between employer and employee, in separate blocks or by reduced working hours; (The Act of 2005 has amended this provision by providing that the fourteen weeks' parental leave may be taken in two separate periods of not less than six weeks each provided that prior to taking the second portion at least ten weeks has elapsed since the end of the first portion).

(iv) the leave is unpaid.

Section 14 addresses the employment position of an employee while absent on parental leave. It provides that:

(i) an employee on parental leave will be treated as if he or she had not been absent so that all his or her employment rights, except the right to remuneration and superannuation benefits, will be unaffected during the leave;

(ii) periods of probation and apprenticeship may be suspended;

(iii) periods of parental leave (and of *force majeure* leave) are not to be reckoned as any other type of leave.

There is an entitlement to return to work on the expiration of a period of parental leave on similar terms as those in s.26 of the Maternity Protection Act 1994 and s.18 of the Adoptive Leave Act 1995 (see s.15, 2005 Act). Where it is not practicable to permit the employee to return to work in accordance with s.15, the employee is entitled to be offered suitable alternative employment (see s.16). As to the meaning of the words "suitable in selection to the employee concerned", see *Tighe v Travenol Laboratories (Ireland) Ltd* (P14/1986), where the EAT said that they should be interpreted "subjectively, from the employee's standpoint, including the general nature of the work which suited her and her domestic considerations."

The Act requires that the leave must be taken as a continuous block.

The leave must be used for the care of a child. The employer has a right to terminate the leave if it is not being used for this purpose. Where the employer does so terminate, the employee must be given seven days' notice of intention to terminate. In these circumstances, the employee is entitled to make representations to the employer.

There is a notification requirement of at least six weeks of intention to take parental leave. The arrangements of the leave are embodied in a document known as a confirmation document which must be signed by both parties at least four weeks before the leave is to be taken. The leave may be postponed by consent even after it has been confirmed. It can be postponed at the option of the employer without the employee's consent only once, and only on the basis that the leave would have substantial adverse effects on the business of the employer. There is an exception in relation to seasonal factors regarding work and where two postponements are permitted. However, there must be consultation between the parties and some reasons for the postponement must be put forward.

Force Majeure Leave

Employees may be entitled to limited leave with pay for family crises (see s.13). Such leave is known as *force majeure* leave and may be availed of in cases where a family member is ill or injured. The maximum *force majeure* leave which may be availed of is three days in 12 consecutive months or five days in 36 consecutive months. An employee who takes *force majeure* leave is required to notify the employer as soon as reasonably practicable and within four weeks to supply to the employer a medical certificate containing particulars of the family member's injury or illness. The notice to be given should be set out in the form in the Schedule to the Parental Leave (Notice of Force Majeure Leave) Regulations 1998 (S.I. No.454 of 1998) or a form to like effect.

The need which requires the taking of *force majeure* leave must be "urgent". Thus, it stands to reason that, if the employee has sufficient advance notice of the need, he or she should make alternative arrangements such as taking a day's holiday. Where an employee takes two or more consecutive day's *force majeure* leave, the statutory qualifications of "urgent", "immediate" and "indispensable" must be present on each of the succeeding days. See *Quinn v J. Higgins*

Engineering Galway Ltd ([2000] E.L.R. 102), where the claimant's wife and children fell ill at a time when there was a meningitis scare in the locality. The claimant took two days off work to take them to a doctor and to mind them thereafter. The EAT found that the claimant's concerns were not unreasonable and that he had "no choice" but to stay off work in order to get medical assistance. Accordingly, he was entitled to *force majeure* leave for the first day but not the second as, although they were ill, the doctor had advised that they were not suffering from meningitis.

Extra consideration should be afforded to single parents and the facts should be looked at from a subjective point of view. In *Carey v Penn Racquet Sports Ltd* ([2001] 3 I.R. 32), the High Court emphasised that questions of urgency and indispensability should not be judged with hindsight. In this case, the plaintiff was a single mother with an eight-year-old child. She had taken a day's leave to look after the child who had woken up with a rash on her legs. The company refused to grant *force majure* leave because, following an examination by the plaintiff's General Practitioner, the child was diagnosed as having a rash which was not serious. The EAT, by a majority, upheld the company's decision but Carroll J. in the High Court was of the opinion that the EAT had erred in law in so deciding saying that the "matter should have been looked at from the plaintiff's point of view at the time the decision was made not to go to work. Also, the plaintiff could not be assumed to have medical knowledge which she did not possess." In the later case of *McGaley v Liebherr Container Cranes Ltd* ([2001] 3 I.R. 563), McCracken J. said that *Carey* was "clear authority that the Tribunal must base its judgment on the facts as they existed at the time of the circumstances which it is alleged gave rise to the implementation" of the provisions of the Act. McCracken J. agreed with Carroll J. that it was an "error of law" to view these circumstances with hindsight and to take into account the ultimate seriousness or otherwise of the illness. McCracken J., however, went on to hold that the question of whether the employee's immediate presence was or was not indispensable was a question of fact to be determined by the Tribunal looking at the circumstances that were known at the time the employee decided to stay at home. As a result of *Carey*, each application for *force majeure* leave must be assessed on a case-by-case basis and a policy approach to this issue could only be general in nature and, therefore, inappropriate for the individual circumstances of each case (see *Dunnes Stores v Hallinan* (PL3/2001)).

Redress

Any dispute or difference between an employee and an employer relating to the entitlements under this Act, as amended, other than a dispute or difference relating to a dismissal, may be referred at first instance by either party not later than six months after the occurrence of the dispute to a Rights Commissioner. There is a right of appeal to the EAT not later than four weeks from the date the decision was given and an appeal to the High Court on a point of law. The EAT may refer a question of law arising in proceedings before it to the High Court for determination by it.

Redress may include either or both of the following:

(a) the grant of parental leave of such length to be taken at such time or times and in such manner as may be so specified,

(b) an award of compensation of such amount as is just and equitable but not exceeding 20 weeks' remuneration in favour of the employee concerned to be paid by the employer concerned.

In *Dunnes Stores v Hallinan,* the claimant was denied *force majeure* leave and was awarded £150 (€190.46) by the Rights Commissioner. The EAT, however, was persuaded that the just and equitable compensation was one day's pay and awarded £54 (€68.57). The EAT did add that it appreciated that a situation might arise in another case where, "because of the inconvenience to the employee or because of aggravating behaviour on the part of the employer, an award greater than the loss could be made".

THE CARER'S LEAVE ACT 2001

This Act, which came into operation on July 2, 2001, confers a right on employees to take temporary unpaid leave from their employment for up to 15 months (65 weeks) to look after persons in need of full-time care and attention. This 65 week period has been extended to 104 weeks by the Social Welfare Law Reform and Pensions Act 2006. An employee, who is entitled to carer's benefit, may engage in limited self-employment within the home or employment outside the home for up to 10 hours a week. He or she may also pursue an educational or training course for up to 10 hours per week.

In addition to the right to take carer's leave, the provisions of the Act protect the employment rights of those employees who avail of the leave over the period of their absence (see s.13). In order to qualify for carer's leave the employee must satisfy the conditions set down in the Act. Failure to qualify for carer's benefit, by not having the necessary PRSI contributions, does not prevent the employee availing of the leave but it will affect any monetary benefit a carer would otherwise receive under the social welfare scheme. Although there is no minimum hours threshold, the employee must have been in the continuous employment of the employer from whose employment the leave is to be taken for at least 12 months before he or she can commence the leave (see s.6). The leave entitlement may be taken as a continuous period or in separate unit periods, the aggregate duration of which does not exceed 104 weeks.

Whereas an employer or employee cannot agree to nullify or exclude the application of the provisions of the Act, there is a provision which allows for the provision of arrangements more favourable than those herein provided.

Protection of employment rights

An employee who is absent from work on carer's leave will be regarded as still working in the employment for all purposes relating to his or her employment and none of his or her rights related to the employment will be affected by availing of carer's leave other than the right to remuneration, certain annual leave, certain public holidays and superannuation benefits.

An employee on carer's leave has a right on termination of carer's leave to return to work (see s.14). The employee is entitled to return to work under the following conditions:

(a) with the employer with whom he or she was working immediately before the start of the period or, where during the employee's absence from work there was or were a change or changes of ownership of the undertaking in which the employee was employed immediately before the absence, the owner on the expiration of the period ("the successor");

(b) in the job that the employee held immediately before the commencement of the period; and

(c) under the contract of employment in respect of which the employee was employed immediately before the commencement of the period or, where a change of ownership such as is referred to in paragraph (a) has occurred, under a contract of employment with the successor, that is identical to the contract under which the employee was employed immediately before such commencement, and (in either case) under terms or conditions not less favourable to the employee than those that would have been applicable to him or her if he or she had not been so absent from work.

Where it is not practicable to permit the employee to return to work in accordance with the above terms, the employee is entitled to be offered suitable alternative employment, again in terms similar to those of s.27 of the Maternity Protection Act 1994, s.19 of the Adoptive Leave Act 1995 and s.16 of the Parental Leave Act 1998.

Redress

An employee may refer a dispute to a Rights Commissioner at first instance not later than six months after the occurrence of the dispute. An appeal lies to the EAT within four weeks of the date on which the decision was communicated to the party. The four week period may be extended up to six weeks (see ss.19, 20 and 21). There is a further appeal on a point of law to the High Court (see s.23). Redress may consist of the granting of carer's leave of such length and at such time as may be specified and the award of compensation of up to 26 weeks' remuneration.

A dispute which relates to whether the person, in respect of whose care the leave is taken, is a person in need of full-time care and attention, is a matter to be resolved pursuant to the Social Welfare legislation.

6. HEALTH, SAFETY AND WELFARE AT WORK

- Health, Safety and Welfare at Work Legislation
- Bullying, Harassment, Sexual Harassment and Victimisation
- Stress in the Workplace

HEALTH, SAFETY AND WELFARE AT WORK LEGISLATION

The national legislative framework regarding the health, safety and welfare at work of employees consists in the main of the Safety, Health and Welfare at Work Act 2005. The 2005 Act expands on some of the provisions in the 1989 Act and makes specific provision for the construction industry. The provisions of other employment law enactments such as the Organisation of Working Time Act 1997, The Maternity Protection Acts, and those of the provisions of the Equality Act 1998 which prohibit harassment and sexual harassment also play a role in the health, safety and welfare of employees.

The National Authority for Occupational Safety and Health was set up under the Act of 1989 and this is the body entrusted with enforcement of the legislative provisions regarding health and safety at work. Notwithstanding the repeal of the 1989 Act, the Authority continues but is now referred to as the Health and Safety Authority.

The Act applies to all employers, self-employed persons and all employees, even trainees and those on work experience. For the purpose of health and safety legislation, a person found at a place of work where work is going on is presumed to be an employee until the contrary is shown. In *Roche v P Kelly & Co. Ltd* ([1969] I.R. 100), it was held by the Supreme Court for the purpose of the machinery guarding provisions in the Factories Act 1955, that "a person employed" included an independent contractor.

Employer's Duties

The duty imposed on employers is set out in s.8. In general terms, the duty imposed on employers is the duty to ensure, so far as is reasonably practicable, the safety, health and welfare at work of all his employees by, *inter alia*, managing and conducting work activities in such a way as to ensure, so far as is reasonably practicable, the safety and health of employees, and managing and conducting work activities in such a manner as would prevent, as far as is reasonably practicable, any improper conduct or behaviour likely to put the safety, health or welfare at work of employees at risk. As regards the place of work, the employer has a duty to ensure so far as is reasonably practicable that the design, provision and maintenance of the place of work is of a condition that is safe and without risk to health. This includes safe means of access and egress from the workplace, and the design and maintenance of plant and machinery. The employer is under a duty to provide a system of work that is planned, organised, performed and maintained so as to be safe and without risk to health. The employer must provide information, instruction, training and supervision as is necessary to ensure the safety and health of employees at work. Where hazards cannot be controlled or eliminated the employer must provide suitable protection such as protective clothing or equipment. The employer must put in place plans for emergencies and the provision of facilities and arrangements for the welfare of employees. Where necessary the employer must engage the services of a competent person for the purpose of ensuring the safety and health at work of employees. The employer is also under a duty to conduct his undertaking in such a way as to ensure, so far as is reasonably practicable, that persons not in his employment but who could be affected are not exposed to risks to their safety or health. An employer must have in place a safety statement.

An employer is under a duty to consult with employees on health and safety issues. Failure to so consult could act to the detriment of the employer where an injury might have been prevented had consultation taken place.

The Act of 2005 expands somewhat on the duties owed by an employer to their employees under the 1989 Act (see s.8). The section specifically refers to "work activities" and requires the employer to manage and conduct "work activities in such a way as to prevent, so far as is reasonably practicable, any improper conduct or behaviour likely to put the safety, health or welfare at work of his or her employees at risk" and to provide and maintain "facilities and arrangements for the welfare of his or her employees at work". This provision may require employers to supply canteen, restroom and refreshment facilities and may even require an employer to provide support systems to employees suffering from stress whether it be from work overload, or bullying and harassment in the workplace. The Act requires employers to ensure that health surveillance appropriate to the risks to safety, health and welfare identified by the risk assessment is made available to employees (see s.22(1)). Health surveillance under the Act means that there must be periodic reviews with the purpose of protecting health and preventing occupational related diseases so that any adverse variations in employees' health, related to working conditions are identified as early as possible. Where there is an accident or hazardous occurrence, an employer is required to report it to the relevant authority (see s.33).

The duty on all self-employed persons is to conduct their business in such a way as to ensure, so far as is reasonably practicable, that he/she and other persons, not being his employees, but who may be affected are not exposed to risks to their safety or health.

The duties under the Act are only imposed where it is "reasonably practicable" or "so far as is reasonably practicable". The 1989 Act contained no definition of "reasonably practicable" and it was left to the courts to come up with a definition and in the main the definition in *Edwards v National Coal Board* [1949] 1 All E.R. 740, was approved. However, the 2005 Act provides a definition of "reasonably practicable" (see s.2(6)). This definition is that an employer must have "exercised all due care by putting in place the necessary protective and preventative measures, having identified the hazards and assessed the risks to safety and health likely to result in accidents or injury to health at the place of work concerned and where the putting in place of any further measures is grossly disproportionate having regard to the unusual, unforeseeable and exceptional nature of any circumstances or occurrence that may result in an accident at work or injury to health at that place of work." This definition encompasses what was identified in *Kirwan v Bray U.D.C.* (unreported, Supreme Court, July 30, 1969) which is that a "slight risk may be run if the cost of remedying it is unreasonably high". However, an employer should proceed with caution on this issue as it will be a court who will decide what "slight" and "unreasonably high" are, should the need arise. The definition also makes it clear that "foreseeability" is a requirement.

Employees' Duties

The employee too has a duty under the Act. The Act frames the duty in terms that the employee is not to "engage in improper conduct or other behaviour that is likely to endanger his or her own safety, health and welfare at work or that of any other person" (see s.13). The use of the words "improper conduct or other behaviour" has the potential to catch such conduct as bullying, harassment and sexual harassment. In general terms, the employee is under a duty to take reasonable care of his/her own personal safety, health and welfare and the safety and health of any other person who may be affected by his acts or omissions while at work. An employee must cooperate with his/her employer by complying with any safety procedures laid down by the employer. He/she must wear protective clothing where and when instructed and must report to his/her employer or supervisor any defects that he/she becomes aware of in plant, equipment, place of work or system of work which might cause danger. Indeed, non-compliance or disregard to any safety procedures may, depending on the gravity of the non-compliance or disregard, justify a dismissal under the Unfair Dismissal Act 1977 because the employer would be dismissing the employee in order to prevent contravention of statute (see s.6(4)(d) of the 1977 Act). Where an employee fails to comply with safety procedures it may be held to be contributory negligence on the part of the employee in a civil action and any compensation awarded may be reduced accordingly (see, for example, *Kennedy v East Cork Foods Ltd* [1973] I.R. 243).

Safety Statement

The safety statement that an employer must have in place is a "proper safety statement" (see s.19). The safety statement must be brought to the attention of the employees at least on an annual basis. The safety statement must be based on the identification of the hazards and risks assessment carried out (see s.20). The safety statement should specify the manner in which safety, health and welfare at work are to be secured. Thus, a safety statement must contain not only the "ends" but the "means" to secure such ends. Failure to prepare a proper safety statement could be used in evidence to the employer's detriment in any civil claim brought by an injured employee. It is specifically required that the safety statement specify the hazards identified and the risks assessed. In *Coffee v Byrne* ([1997] E.L.R. 230), the EAT held that failure to carry out a risk assessment meant there was insufficient compliance with the provisions of the 1989 Act.

Codes of Practice

The Health and Safety Authority is required to prepare and issue codes of practice. Codes of Practice are not legally binding but they can be admitted in legal proceedings in the ordinary courts and in tribunals. Further, an employer's failure to have regard to them can be detrimental to any defence (see *Browne v Ventlo Telecommunications (Ireland) Ltd* (UD 597/2001)).

Inspectors

Under the legislation there is provision for Inspectors who have powers to carry out tours of inspection of places of work, such powers including the power to enter, inspect, examine and search both the workplace and equipment and machinery (see ss.62 and 64).

Offences

There is provision for prosecution of offences under the Act. The most common form of prosecution is by summary proceedings in the District Court. Where the breach is more serious the matter will be dealt with on indictment. In any proceedings for an offence where the duty or requirement to do something in "so far as is practicable" or "so far as is reasonably practicable", the onus of proof will be on the accused. Although the Act is essentially a criminal and penalising statute, an injured employee is not precluded from maintaining a civil action for breach of statutory duty.

THE COMMON LAW

Employers also have a common law duty of care to their employees (see *Wilsons & Clyde Coal Company v English* ([1938] A.C. 57)). The scope of the duty owed by employers to their employees has been analysed by the courts under four general headings, *viz.* the provision of competent staff, the provision of a safe place of work, the provision of proper equipment and the provision of a safe system of work (see discussion in McMahon and Binchy in *Irish Law of Torts*) (see, for example, *O'Donnell v Hannigan* (unreported, Supreme Court, July 19, 1960)). Breach of this duty may result in an employer being liable for personal injury including psychiatric injury (*Frost v Chief Constable of South Yorkshire* ([1999] 2 A.C. 455) and *Curran v Cadbury (Irl) Ltd* ([2000] 2 I.L.R.M. 343)). However, see *Fletcher v The Commissioners of Public Works in Ireland* ([2003] 2 I.L.R.M. 94) where the psychiatric injury complained of was held to be too remote (unforeseeable) and was in the nature of an irrational fear.

Employers may also be vicariously liable for the actions of their employees which cause injuries to third parties, such as other employees or other persons. In general, the courts impose liability on an employer for the torts of his/her employees if they are committed within the scope of the employment (see, for example, *Kiely v McCrea & Sons Ltd* ([1940] Ir. Jur. Rep. 1)). For a more detailed treatment of employer's liability in tort and employer's vicarious liability in tort see *Irish Law of Torts* (McMahon & Binchy, Butterworth (Ireland) Ltd, Dublin).

Claims by employees against their employers for personal injury at work or work related personal injury must firstly be referred to the Personal Injuries Assessment Board (PIAB). The role of PIAB in employers' liability claims, like other personal injury claims, will be confined to claims which the employer accepts are genuine and where liability is admitted by the employer. PIAB do not conduct oral hearings. Assessment of claims are made on a documents-only (including medical reports) system. Where liability is not admitted by the employer, claims may be litigated in the usual manner through the courts.

BULLYING, HARASSMENT, SEXUAL HARASSMENT AND VICTIMISATION

It has long been recognised that bullying, harassment and, in particular, sexual harassment can have a devastating effect upon the health, confidence, morale and performance of those affected by it and where an employee suffers injury such as illness, either physical or psychological, as a result of such treatment an action may lie in tort for such injury. In *Reilly v Bonny* (*Irish Times*, November 20, 1997) and in *Smith v Tanner* (Irish Times, November 4, 2003), it was held that sexual harassment amounted to a tort. See also *Curran v Cadbury (Irl) Ltd* [2000] 2 I.L.R.M. 343, where the Circuit Court held that the duty to avoid injury included both physical and mental injury, even where the employer foresees physical injury only.

Bullying, victimisation, harassment, including sexual harassment are prohibited conduct in the workplace and can lead to actions under the equality legislation for discrimination (*viz*. Employment Equality Act 1998 and Equality Act 2004) or under the health and safety legislation (Safety, Health and Welfare at Work Act 2005). See *Atkinson v Carthy* ([2005] E.L.R. 1), where the judge said that "an employer is obliged to provide a safe place of work, a safe system of work and a safe working environment. The onus is on the employer by law to provide for same". See also *Quigley v Complex Tooling and Moulding* (unreported, High Court, March 9, 2005), where it was held that employers now have an obligation under health and safety legislation to prevent their employees from such that would cause mental injury like stress. Employers are under a duty to act in a preventative and remedial way regarding harassment and sexual harassment. Unless an employer can demonstrate that he/she took reasonable steps to prevent bullying, harassment or sexual harassment, the employer will be vicariously liable. To rely on such a defence, an employer would need to demonstrate that he/she had a comprehensive, accessible and effective policy on harassment and sexual harassment in place. Best practice would indicate that such a policy should focus on prevention and contain an effective complaints procedure with remedial action taken wherever appropriate.

A discriminatory action may arise if the prohibited treatment is meted out to an employee as a result of their belonging to one of the nine categories set out in s.6 of the Employment Equality Act *viz.* because of the employee's gender, marital status, family status, sexual orientation, religion, age, race, membership of the Traveller community or because the employee in question is disabled.

Where there is bullying and harassment, including sexual harassment, there will be a victim and a perpetrator. In the workplace, the victim will almost always be an employee whereas the perpetrator may be a fellow employee, colleague, the employer, an employment agency, clients or customers of the business or any person who has reason to visit the business or undertaking at the employer's behest. On this latter category, see *A Company v A Worker* (EE03/1991 reported at [1992] E.L.R. 40), where the perpetrator was an invitee who had permission to be on the company premises for his own business purposes. Thus, an employer may be vicariously liable for acts of bullying, harassment and sexual harassment not only of its employees but also of those with whom it deals in the course of its business and where the employer is a school. It may also be vicariously liable for acts of bullying, harassment and sexual harassment of its students (see, for example, *Two Named Female Teachers and the Equality Authority v Board of Management and Principal of a Boys' Secondary School* ([2001] E.L.R. 159)). However, an employer will only be held vicariously liable in circumstances where he knew or ought to have known of the harassment. Where both parties are employees, the employer must afford fair procedures to *both* parties.

Harassment and Sexual Harassment in the Workplace

Harassment and sexual harassment are now defined in statute (see s.8 of the Equality Act 2004 which replaced s.23 of the Employment Equality Act 1998). What type of conduct amounts to bullying, harassment and sexual harassment may also be defined in documents of the employer company such as policy documents on bullying, harassment and sexual harassment. In *Michael Foley v Aer Lingus Plc* ([2001] E.L.R. 193), a case which involved allegations of sexual harassment, the plaintiff's conduct was measured by a committee comprising of members of the Board of Directors against the Respect and Dignity in the Workplace document of the defendant company (see also *Browne v Ventelo Telecommunications*).

Section 8 of the 2004 Act defines harassment as follows:

"Where an unwanted conduct related to the sex of a person occurs for the purpose or effect of violating the dignity of a person and of creating an intimidating, hostile, degrading, humiliating or offensive environment;"

Section 8 defines sexual harassment as follows:

"Where any form of unwanted verbal, non verbal or physical conduct of a sexual nature occurs, with the purpose or effect of violating the dignity of a person, in particular when creating an intimidating, hostile, degrading, humiliating or offensive environment."

Section 8(7) goes on to provide that references to harassment refer "to any form of unwanted conduct relating to any of the discriminatory grounds, and references to sexual harassment refer to any form of unwanted verbal, non verbal or physical conduct of a sexual nature, being conduct which in either case has the purpose of [*sic*] effect of violating a person's dignity and creating an intimidating, hostile, and degrading, humiliating or offensive environment for the person and includes such unwanted conduct as acts, requests, spoken words, gestures or the production, display or circulation of written words, pictures or other material".

Section 23 of the 1998 Act specifically required that both the conduct in question must be unwelcome to the victim and must also reasonably be regarded on the gender ground as sexually or otherwise offensive, humiliating or intimidating to them. The removing of the "reasonableness" requirement by the 2004 Act means that the conduct is to be judged subjectively and that it is for the victim alone to decide what is unwanted conduct, and whether or not the conduct violates their dignity or creates an intimidating, hostile, degrading, humiliating or offensive environment. In *Allen v Independent Newspapers (Ireland) Ltd* (UD641/2000), the EAT said that an employee's perception that they have been subjected to a hostile working environment must be "reasonable".

Whereas the prohibited behaviour must occur in the workplace, workplace is defined as a place where the employee/victim is or any place the employee/victim is otherwise in the course of their employment. It can also include a place of socialising when such socialising is work-related. For example, the "office party", work-related events or social or business functions, consultations, conferences, seminars, meetings irrespective of the venue or *locus*, or other sports and social outings where employees congregate. These events do not necessarily have to be formally organised or arranged by the employer.

Sexual Harassment

In addition to the conduct listed in s.8(7) of the Act of 2004, the *Code of Practice on Sexual Harassment and Harassment at Work* (Published by the Equality Authority, Dublin, 2002) gives as examples of prohibited conduct constituting harassment and sexual harassment, touching, patting, pinching, brushing against another employee's body, assault, coercive sexual intercourse, unwelcome sexual advances, unwelcome propositions, unwelcome pressure for sexual activity, continued suggestions for social activity outside of the workplace after it has been made clear that such suggestions are unwelcome, unwanted or offensive flirtations and suggestive remarks, lewd innuendo and comments, display of pornographic or sexually suggestive pictures, display of pornographic or sexually suggestive objects, display of pornographic or sexually suggestive written materials, display of pornographic or sexually suggestive e-mails, display of pornographic or sexually suggestive faxes, display of pornographic or sexually suggestive text messages. In addition, conduct which is discriminatory, derogatory or which denigrates, ridicules or is intimidatory or which is physically or mentally abusive and which is visited upon a person because of his/her gender, may constitute sexual harassment. See, for example, *Two Named Female Teachers and the Equality Authority v Board of Management and Principal of a Boys' Secondary School* [2001] E.L.R. 159), where the conduct, which was held to be sexual harassment, included the attaching of a lewd and sexually offensive note to the back of a female teacher's back by male pupils, and whistling and name-calling of a sexually offensive nature directed at female members of staff.

The Labour Court in *A Worker v A Garage Proprietor* (EE02/ 1985) ruled that "freedom from sexual harassment is a condition of work which an employee of either sex is entitled to expect". Sexual harassment is a broad category of offence and comprises conduct of varying degrees of seriousness. See *James Allen v Dunnes Stores Ltd* ([1996] E.L.R. 203), where the conduct complained of included commenting on the perfume a female employee was wearing and attempting to kiss her, standing under the stairs as the female staff went upstairs, commenting on the amount of tights a female member of staff bought and enquiring how they ripped. The test as to what constitutes sexual harassment is subjective. Whether behaviour amounts to sexual harassment in a particular instance is determined from the point of view of the victim and what she/he regards as acceptable behaviour. Behaviour regarded as acceptable and innocent by the perpetrator, his colleagues and others, may nonetheless be unacceptable to the victim and so may constitute "sexual harassment". The onus is on the employer to put in place a programme to inform, educate and instruct employees on the issue of sexual harassment (see s.8(7) of the 2004 Act and *Allen v Dunnes Stores Ltd*).

Thus, the essential characteristic of sexual harassment is that it is unwanted by the recipient (s.8(7) of the 2004 Act and *A Company v A Worker* ([1990] E.L.R. 187)). Section 23 of the 1998 Act (now replaced by s.8 of the 2004 Act) ascribed a wide ambit to the concept of "sexual harassment" and drew heavily on the European Commission's Code of Practice on measures to combat sexual harassment ([1992] O.J. C49/1) and the Department of Equality and Law Reform's Code of Practice on Measures to Protect the Dignity of Women and Men at Work (1994). In the Commission's Code of Practice, sexual harassment is defined as "unwanted conduct of a sexual nature or other conduct based on sex affecting the dignity of women and men at work". The focus is now very much on how the conduct was regarded by the recipient rather than on the motive or intention of the perpetrator. Note that whereas the provisions of the Code of Practice are admissible in evidence, they do not in and of themselves impose any legal obligations.

Sexual harassment may take place outside the workplace: see *A Limited Company v One Female Employee* (EE10/1988), where the alleged harassment occurred during a residential company training programme in a hotel.

Harassment

Harassment is any act or conduct by the alleged perpetrator including, but not limited to spoken words, gestures or the production, display or circulation of written words, pictures or other material if the action or other conduct is unwelcome to the victim and could reasonably be regarded, in relation to the relevant characteristic of the victim as offensive, humiliating or intimidating (s.8 of the 2004 Act). Prohibited conduct would be conduct that is derogatory or imtimidatory or conduct which denigrates or ridicules. Harassment of an employee based on any of the non-gender grounds set out in s.6 of the Employment Equality Act 1998 (marital status, family status, age, sexual orientation, religious beliefs, race, member of the Traveller community or because of a disability) constitutes discrimination. Conversely, treating an employee in a discriminatory manner based on any of the grounds set out in s.9 constitutes harassment. See, for example, in *A Named Female v A Named Company* (DEC-E 2002/014), where harassment on grounds of age was held to have occurred where an employee of the respondent frequently and in a derogatory manner made references to the age and inexperience of the claimant, specifically telling the claimant that she was "only a young foolish girl more inexperienced than he". In *Francis Maguire v North Eastern Health Board* (DEC-E-2002/39), the impugned conduct on the Traveller ground included fellow workers bossing the claimant around and telling him what to do and telling him to do their work, being disturbed at rest breaks to do some tasks while fellow workers were never so disturbed, being asked to sign a three month contract after it was discovered he was a member of the Traveller community, being called a knacker, kicking him, attacking him, being reprimanded in a humiliating manner and being isolated by fellow workers at social functions.

Victimisation

Victimisation can include, *inter alia*, penalising employees for referring their complaints to the appropriate authority. An example of victimisation includes encouraging staff not directly involved in a referral to attend at the hearing (see *Two Named Female Teachers and the Equality*

Authority v Board of Management and Principal of a Boys' Secondary School). It can include reducing the working hours allocated to the complainant after he/she made a complaint to a relevant authority (see *Francis Maguire v North Eastern Health Board*).

In *Jacqui McCarthy v Dublin Corporation* ([2001] E.L.R.255), a case concerning an allegation of bullying and victimisation, the alleged facts being that: the manager did not speak to the complainant; his attitude in dealing with the complainant; the inaccurate reporting of the Labour Court determination at a management meeting—the minutes of which were published internally—and the subsequent refusal of the respondent to correct the minutes; and the manner in which the investigation into claims of bullying and harassment against the complainant was conducted. The Equality Officer concluded the complainant had established a prima facie case of victimisation in that she was penalised for having previously brought a claim under the equality legislation, which the respondent had failed to rebut.

Fair Procedures for Investigations of Bullying and Harassment, including Sexual Harassment

Fair procedures must be afforded to all parties. Fair procedures include that the parties should be informed of the procedure regarding investigation, and they should be informed of their right to be accompanied by a trade union representative, a friend or colleague. Confidentiality should be maintained. Specifically, the perpetrator has:

- The right to be told what the problem is.
- The right to make representations.
- The right to be heard.
- Where appropriate, a right to make a plea in mitigation.
- If a decision is to be made, a right to be informed of that decision in advance and once the decision has been taken, a right to be informed of the decision.

In *A Named Female v A Named Company* (DEC-E 2002/014), the respondent was held to have breached the principle of fair procedures because its investigation process was neither fair nor equitable in that the complainant was asked for written statements, whereas the alleged perpetrator was afforded the opportunity of meeting the board and replying orally. The complainant was not given an opportunity to make oral submissions or to respond to the statements of the alleged perpetrator.

STRESS IN THE WORKPLACE

Where stress is caused in the workplace either as a result of pressure of work, harassment, including sexual harassment, bullying, victimisation or otherwise, it may be actionable either under common law principles or under health and safety legislation (see *Walker v Northumberland Co. Co.* ([1995] I.C.R. 702)). That work-related stress is actionable under the health and safety legislation is clear from the decision in *McGrath v Trintech Technologies Limited and Trintech Group Plc* ([2005] E.L.R. 49), where the court stated it had no difficulty with the argument that the 1989 Act and the Safety, Health and Welfare at Work (General Applications) Regulations 1993 covered injury for psychiatric health and psychiatric injuries.

Stress can also result from overwork. In *Sullivan v Southern Health Board* ([1997] 3 I.R. 123), the plaintiff was a medical consultant employed by the defendant health board. He claimed that he was overworked. It was held that the plaintiff was entitled to compensation for stress and anxiety caused to him, in both his professional and domestic life, by the persistent failure of the Board to remedy his complaints. See also the English case of *Young v PO* ([2002 I.R.L.R. 660), where the plaintiff employee had two episodes of breakdown due to stress. Prior to the plaintiff's return, the first-time promises were made but these were not kept and the plaintiff suffered a second episode. The defendant raised the argument that the plaintiff had a duty to advise his employer that he was unable to cope and that his failure to so advise the employer was such that the employer could not be expected to be aware of the plight that he was in. That argument was rejected by the Court of Appeal, as it was clear that the plaintiff, following his return from stress-related leave, was vulnerable and the promises made by the employer to remedy the situation were not kept and thus the employer was in breach of a duty (see also *Sutherland v Hatton* ([2002] I.T.L.R. 263) and the *Liz Allen* case).

Notwithstanding, there is a positive duty on an employee to advise his employer of difficulties, and certainly where an employer makes an inquiry of an employee following a period of absence and is told that there is no work-related problem, then generally, the employer will be entitled to take this at face value. An employer is not obliged to be inspired. It is only where the employer knows or ought reasonably to have known that there was stress, be it from overwork, harassment or bullying or otherwise, that the employer's failure to act will constitute a breach of duty. There is an element of subjectivity in this test. The employer is not entitled to judge all employees equally. Nor is the employer entitled to assume that all employees are of reasonable fortitude. Instead, the test extrapolated from the *Sutherland v Hatton* case is whether a harmful reaction to the pressures of the work was reasonably foreseeable in the individual concerned. Medical evidence may support a finding of stress and the facts may support a finding that it was caused by work-related events but, nonetheless, if it was not reasonably foreseeable by the employer that the events would cause such a reaction (stress), then a plaintiff will fail in their action. Where an employer knows or suspects an employee is suffering from stress, he should consider the provision of a sabbatical, counselling, monitoring, supervision by a senior employee or the provision of extra systems and support.

An employee can also suffer a stress-related injury—psychological or physical—as a result of the manner in which a dismissal was effected and may claim damages for this as distinct from damages for the dismissal itself (see the English case of *Gogay v Hartfordshire County Council* ([2000] I.R.L.R. 703)). This case should be looked at in tandem with *Johnson v Unisys* ([1999] I.R.L.R. 90). However, damages will not be awarded for injury due to hurt feelings arising out of the manner of the dismissal. There must be something more. See *Addis v Gramaphone Co.* ([1909] A.C. 488), a House of Lords decision, where it was found that there was a psychological injury rather than mere hurt feelings. In *O'Byrne v Dunnes Stores* (High Court, October 24, 2002), damages were awarded in the context of wrongful dismissal, which appeared to have taken account of stress (see also *Carey v Independent Newspapers* ([2004] 3 I.R. 52)).

7. TERMINATION OF THE EMPLOYMENT CONTRACT

The main ways of terminating the contract of employment are, from the employer's perspective, dismissal (including dismissal by reason of redundancy or dismissal due to the employer's insolvency) or in the case of a fixed-term contract, efflux of time. The transfer of an undertaking, business or part of a business does not of itself constitute grounds for dismissal and is prohibited (Reg.5 of the Transfer of Undertakings Regulations 2003). From the employee's perspective, the main way of terminating the contract of employment is by resignation. An employment contract may also be terminated by retirement of the employee or by the death of either party. Additionally, the contract may be terminated or discharged under the general principles and rules of contract law.

The Unfair Dismissal Acts 1977–1993

The principal Act, which came into operation on May 9, 1977, has been amended and modified by the later Acts and has had sections inserted into it by virtue of various other enactments. The principal Act varied the common law position which held that so long as the appropriate contractual notice, or wages in lieu, was given, an employer was free to dismiss an employee for whatever reason.

The 1977 Act starts with a presumption that a dismissal is unfair unless there are substantial grounds justifying that dismissal and the onus lies on the employer to rebut that presumption. The EAT has consistently held that whether the employer has demonstrated that there were substantial grounds justifying the dismissal and thus rebutting the presumption is to be answered by applying an objective standard, *viz.* the way in which a reasonable employer, in those circumstances and in that line of business, would have behaved (see, for example, *Bunyan v United Dominions Trust (Ireland) Ltd* ([1982] I.L.R.M. 404) and *Looney & Co. Ltd v Looney* (UD 843/1984)).

The Act also established mechanisms whereby claims of unfair dismissal may be investigated impartially, cheaply and relatively informally.

Excluded Employees

Employees with less than one year's service are excluded. There are, however, some significant exceptions to this rule, such as where the dismissal is for reasons of trade union membership, pregnancy or maternity or adoptive leave. Where the dismissal is solely or mainly for reasons connected therewith, there is no minimum service requirement at all. Also excluded is an employee who has reached normal retiring age for employees in similar employment or who has reached the age of 65 years of age; a person employed by a family member in a home or farm where both employer and employee reside; or members of An Garda Síochána, the Defence Forces and Officers of various other State/semi-State organisations as well as FÁS trainees, statutory apprentices; and persons on fixed term or specified purpose contracts (but on this latter category see the Protection of Employees (Fixed-Term Work Act) 2003. Civil servants had been an excluded category but since the implementation of the Civil Service Regulations (Amendment) Act 2005, the application of the Unfair Dismissals Acts 1977–2001 has been extended to this category of worker. An apprentice, not excluded from the Act, must have 12 months' service (see *Moore v Donegal County* UD 839/1998). If a probationary period extends beyond 12 months, that probationary employee falls within the provisions of the Acts (see *Keating v Bus Éireann* (UD 680/2001)).

Notwithstanding that an employer may not dismiss on the basis that a worker is a fixed-term contract worker, an employer can avail of a fixed-term or specified purpose contract and the Acts will not apply when the term expires or the purpose ceases (see s.2(2)(a)). However, four conditions must be satisfied. The contract must:

(1) be in writing;
(2) must be signed by or on behalf of the employer;
(3) must be signed by the employee;
(4) must provide that the Unfair Dismissals Act 1977 shall not apply to a dismissal consisting only of the expiry of the fixed term or the cesser of the specified purpose (see *Sheehan v Dublin Tribune Ltd* ([1992] E.L.R. 239) and *O'Connor v Kilnamanagh Family Recreation Centre Ltd* (UD 1102/1993)).

Provided the employee has the requisite service, there is nothing to prevent a claim being made in respect of a dismissal during the continuance of the fixed term. Where an employee is dismissed at the expiry of a fixed-term contract and is re-employed within three months under another fixed-term contract and the employee is then dismissed by reason of the expiry of the second or subsequent fixed-term contract, the terms of the various contracts can be added together and will be deemed to be continuous service (Unfair Dismissals (Amendment) Act 1993). This is, however, conditional on it being found that the entry into the subsequent contracts was for the purpose of avoiding liability under the Act (see *Kierse v National University of Ireland, Galway* (UD 219/2000)). However, the employer may still be able to show that there were substantial grounds justifying the dismissal (see *Fitzgerald v St. Patrick's College Maynooth* (UD 244/1978)).

Dismissal

As stated above, the contract of employment may be brought to an end by a dismissal. A dismissal may be actual or constructive. A constructive dismissal is where the employee leaves their employment because circumstances were such that he/she could no longer endure the situation at work. In effect, the employer's behaviour is such that it constitutes a repudiation of the contract of employment. Behaviour that has been held to amount to repudiation by an employer includes unilateral reduction of the remuneration of the employee and changing the agreed workplace to somewhere unsuitable because of distance. The 1977 Act specifically recognises the concept of constructive dismissal in that the Act provides that "the termination by the employee of his contract of employment with his employer, whether prior notice of the termination was or was not given to the employer, in circumstances in which, because of the conduct of the employer, the employee was or would have been entitled, or it was or would have been reasonable for the employee, to terminate the contract of employment without giving prior notice of the termination to the employer" (see s.1(1)(b)). This definition means that there are two alternative tests for proving a constructive dismissal:

(1) the employee was entitled to resign; or
(2) it was reasonable for the employee to resign.

In cases of constructive dismissal, the onus lies on the claimant to prove what has happened amounted to a dismissal. Only when this is established will an assessment of whether the dismissal was fair or unfair be carried out (see, for example, *Cantor Fitzgerald International v Callaghan* [1999] I.C.R. 639 and *Allen v Independent Newspapers (Ireland) Ltd* (UD641/2000)).

Dismissals—Fair and Unfair

A dismissal must not be unfair or wrongful. As to whether a dismissal is unfair or not, the dismissal must be assessed through the prism of the Unfair Dismissal Acts 1977–1993 and a wrongful dismissal will be assessed against common law rules and principles.

Dismissals are categorised in the Act as those that are "fair" and those that are "unfair" (ss.6(2) and 6(4)). In dismissals deemed unfair, the employee bears the burden of proof whereas in dismissals deemed fair the employer bears the burden of proof. The EAT has taken the view that the Act merely sets out potentially fair reasons which might justify a dismissal with a more general area of justification provided in the form of "other substantial grounds". There is, at best, only a prima facie justification and the substance of such justification will be enquired into by the EAT (see *Durnin v Building & Engineering Co. Ltd* (UD 159/1978)).

Dismissals Automatically Deemed Unfair

Section 6 of the Act provides that the dismissal of an employee will be deemed, for the purposes of the Act, to be an unfair dismissal if it results wholly or mainly from one or more of the following:

(a) the employee's membership, or proposal that he or another person become a member of, or his engaging in activities on behalf of, a trade union or excepted body under the Trade Union Acts 1941 and 1971, as amended by the Industrial Relations Act 1990, where the times at which he engages in such activities are outside his hours of work or are times during his hours of work in which he is permitted, pursuant to the contract of employment between him and his employer, to so engage;

(b) the religious or political opinions of the employee;

(c) civil proceedings whether actual, threatened or proposed against the employer to which the employee is or will be a party or in which the employee was or is likely to be a witness;

(d) criminal proceedings against the employer, whether actual, threatened or proposed, in relation to which the employee has made, proposed or threatened to make a complaint or statement to the prosecuting authority or to any other authority connected with or involved in the prosecution of the proceedings or in which the employee was or is likely to be a witness;

(dd) the exercise or proposed exercise by the employee of the right to parental leave, *force majeure* leave under and in accordance with the Parental Leave Act 1998, or carer's leave under and in accordance with the Carer's Leave Act 2001;

(e) the race, colour or sexual orientation of the employee;

(ee) the age of the employee;

(eee) the employee's membership of the Traveller community;

(f) the employee's pregnancy, giving birth or breastfeeding or any matters connected therewith;

(g) the exercise or proposed exercise by the employee of a right under the Maternity Protection Act 1994 to any form of protective leave or natal care absence, within the meaning of Part IV of that Act;

(h) the exercise or contemplated exercise by an adopting parent of her right under the Adoptive Leave Act 1995 to adoptive leave or additional adoptive leave.

An employee is deemed to be dismissed and the dismissal shall be deemed to be an unfair dismissal if, after the termination of a lock-out or following the taking part in a strike or other industrial action, the employee is not permitted to resume his employment on terms and conditions at least as favourable to the employee and one or more other employees in the same employment were so permitted (s.5). Such dismissals are subject to the general presumption of unfairness established by s.6(1) of the 1977 Act (see *Tuke v Coillte Teoranta* ([1998] E.L.R. 324) and *Folan v Dunnes Stores (Terryland) Ltd* (UD56/ 2000)). Where an employee, who is entitled to return to work following absence on "protective leave"—under such Acts as the Maternity Protection Act or the Adoptive Leave Act—but is not permitted to, that employee is deemed to have been dismissed on the expected date of return and the dismissal is deemed to be an unfair dismissal unless, having regard to all the circumstances, there were substantial grounds justifying the dismissal. An employee who is dismissed for exercising his/her rights under the National Minimum Wage Act is deemed to be unfairly dismissed. A dismissal due to redundancy is deemed to be an unfair dismissal if the claimant has been unfairly selected for redundancy (see *Lynch v Baily* (UD 837/1994)).

Where a dismissal is deemed to be unfair, the onus shifts to the employee to show that the dismissal was wholly or mainly for one of the reasons set out above (see *Reid v Oxx* (1986) 4 I.L.T. 207). The issue as to the onus of proof in alleged pregnancy-related dismissals was fully considered in *Pedreschi v Burke* (UD 591/1999), where the EAT held that, in such a case, the claimant bore the onus of proof. However, in the case of a dismissal due to a redundancy, the onus lies on the employer to show that the selection was fair (see *Caladom Ltd v Hoard and Kelly,* Circuit Court, November 8, 1985).

Dismissals Deemed to be Fair

A dismissal shall not be unfair if it results wholly or mainly from one or more of the following reasons:

(a) The capacity, competence or qualifications of the employee.

(b) The conduct of the employee.

(c) The redundancy of the employee.

(d) The employee being unable to work or continue to work in the position which he held without contravention (by him or by his employer) of a duty or restriction imposed by or under any statute or instrument made under statute.

(e) Other substantial grounds.

The procedure used prior to the dismissal in these circumstances must also be fair. In determining whether the dismissal was unfair or not, it will be for the employer to show that there were substantial grounds justifying the dismissal and thus the burden of proof is, in this respect, firmly on the employer. The employer must show that the dismissal resulted wholly or mainly from one or more of the matters specified at (a)–(d) above, or that there were other substantial grounds justifying the dismissal. It would be a gross mistake, however, for an employer to presume that because you have a ground that fits into one of these four categories that by itself is sufficient to justify the dismissal. In order to succeed, the employer must demonstrate that the incapacity, incompetence or misconduct was the actual reason for the dismissal and that fair procedures were followed prior to the dismissal (see *Bolger v Showerings (Ireland) Ltd* ([1990] E.L.R. 184)).

Capacity

Where an employee is dismissed because of his/her lack of capacity for the job, the dismissal may be justified and may thus be lawful. Capacity would appear to mean that the employee becomes unfit in the course of the employment to carry out the tasks for which he/she was hired. An employer is not necessarily required to find alternative work and reassign an incapacitated employee (see *Cummins v Jury* ([1994] E.L.R. 21)). An employer would be required to show, by way of medical evidence or otherwise, that the employee is so unfit. Any such conclusion reached by an employer should only be reached following fair procedures. In *Bolger v Showerings,* where an employee was dismissed due to incapacity, it was held that in order for an employer to show that the dismissal was fair, the employer must show that:

(1) it was the ill-health which was the reason for his dismissal;
(2) that this was substantial reason;
(3) the employee received fair notice that the question of his dismissal for incapacity was being considered; and
(4) the employee was afforded an opportunity of being heard.

Competence

If you do not hold the qualifications you should have for the job for which employed, that may be grounds for dismissal. If an employee's competence is in issue, clearly it is unfair to make a decision without allowing the employee to address the particular difficulty. Again, the most important thing is that the employee is told of his/her lacking and perhaps reach an agreement with the employer that he/she should improve. If training is required, then it should be given. A warning should be given in situations where competence or conduct is in issue. In giving the warning, the following principles might be borne in mind:

- the warning must be clear;
- it must be clear as to why the warning is being administered;

- it must be clear as to how the employee's performance is expected to improve (performance or conduct);
- where support is required or where targets are to be met, or both, this should be clearly stated in the warning; and
- most importantly, it must be made absolutely clear what the consequences of failure to improve will be.

See *O'Donoghoe v Emerson (Ireland) Ltd* (EAT, 1986 reported in *Dismissal Law in Ireland,* Mary Redmond, Butterworths, Dublin 1999), where the EAT was satisfied that the employer, far from giving the claimant a clear warning instead made an "off-the-cuff" comment. Such "off-the-cuff" comments, a scolding or series of scoldings is not sufficient to constitute a warning. There is an obligation on the employer, where the competence of an employee is in question, to update itself on that employee's performance before taking the decision to dismiss (see *O'Brien v Professional Contract Cleaners Ltd* ([1991] E.L.R. 143)).

Misconduct

Misconduct will usually refer to behaviour during the hours of work. However, it may refer to behaviour engaged in by the employee outside working hours. Where there is a dismissal resulting from an allegation of misconduct, the EAT will examine all the facts and decide whether the penalty of dismissal was justified in the circumstances. The EAT will not generally supplant its own opinion for that of the employer but rather will consider whether the employee had been made aware and had adequate opportunity to deny the allegations or explain the circumstances before the decision to dismiss was taken. The EAT will consider whether the employer believed that the employee had conducted himself or herself as alleged; whether the employer had reasonable grounds to sustain that belief; and whether the penalty of dismissal was proportionate to the alleged misconduct. The general approach of the EAT in cases of dismissals for misconduct is set out in *Hennessy v Read & Write Shop Ltd* (UD 192/1978), where it was held that in deciding whether or not the dismissal of the claimant was unfair, a test of reasonableness should be applied. Matters to be examined include the nature and extent of the enquiry carried out by the employer prior to the decision to dismiss and the conclusion arrived at by the employer that, on the basis of the information resulting from such enquiry, the claimant should be dismissed. The employer, thus, will be required to establish not only that it had substantial grounds justifying dismissal but also that it followed fair and proper procedures. See *Frizelle v New Ross Credit Union Ltd* (unreported, High Court, July 30, 1997), where the court said "put very simply, principles of natural justice must be unequivocally applied".

As to whether the employer had reasonable grounds for believing that the employee was guilty of misconduct, see *Bergin v Dublin Bus* (UD 1987), where the claimant employee was dismissed for an assault on a fellow employee but five times that day, prior to the assault, the claimant had sought to be relieved from duty due to ill health. Following the incident, he produced a medical certificate showing that he was on a considerable amount of medication. The EAT held that these were mitigating circumstances and indicated that the problem was a medical one rather than a straightforward issue of misconduct. The dismissal was held to be unfair and reinstatement was ordered. In *Preston v Standard Piping Ltd* [1999] E.L.R. 233 UD 960/97 NIN 1830/97, an unfair dismissal case, there was an allegation of theft of copper piping. The claimant was summoned to a meeting and was not told it was a disciplinary meeting and no details were given to him at this meeting as to who had made the allegations or when the theft occurred. The claimant was given the opportunity to resign or be dismissed. His claim of unfair dismissal was upheld and compensation was awarded on the basis that the employer had failed to act in compliance with the requirements of natural and constitutional justice. The evidence was merely that copper piping was seen in his van and the employer failed to ask why it was there and whether it was stolen at all.

As stated above, conduct outside the workplace may be relevant and may constitute a valid ground for dismissal where the conduct in question would have an impact on the working relationship, by reason of damaging the bond of trust and confidence or where the conduct in question might undermine the ethos or reputation of the employee. See *Flynn v Power* ([1985] I.R. 648), which concerned a teacher in a Catholic school who was dismissed because she was living with a married man and became pregnant. It was held by the court that a religious school was entitled to take into account its aims and objectives which differ from those of a secular institution and to conclude that the claimant's behaviour amounted to the rejection of the religious tenets which the school wanted to promote. The Equality Act specifically permits discrimination on the basis of religion where it is done to preserve the religious ethos. In *Noone v Dunnes Stores*

Mullingar Ltd (unreported, Circuit Court, July 14, 1989 (UD/1988)), the claimant was convicted of assaulting a Garda and of being drunk and a danger to traffic and as a result, she was dismissed. The EAT did not think the offences were sufficiently serious to warrant her dismissal because the EAT was not convinced that the employer's interests were prejudiced by the adverse publicity. In the same year, the case of *Martin v Dunnes Enniscorthy Ltd* (UD 571/1988) was heard. Here, the dismissed employee was convicted of breaking and entering and committing a larceny. The EAT held that because the claimant was working in a retail store and whilst trust is an essential ingredient in the employer/employee relationship it is so *a fortiori* in relation to a retail store, and the dismissal was thus justified.

Contravention of Statute
A dismissal will be justified where to continue with the employment would be in contravention of a statute, s.6.2.4(d) of the Unfair Dismissals Act 1977. In *Brennan v Blue Gas* (UD 591/1993, *Unfair Dismissals, Cases & Commentary,* Kerr & Madden, Employers' Confederation, Dublin, 1996) a truck driver was dismissed because the employer, despite making exhaustive efforts, could not obtain insurance either for the claimant or other employees due to the bad accident record of the claimant. This dismissal was upheld as not being an unfair dismissal.

Other Substantial Grounds Justifying a Dismissal
In *McSweeney v OK Garages Ltd* (UD 107/1978), *Unfair Dismissals, Cases & Commentary,* Kerr & Madden), which concerned a fight between the workers and members of the same Union, the employer dismissed the minority—consisting of four employees—on the basis that it had no choice and the decision was made in circumstances of the interests of industrial peace. Those dismissals were held to be unfair dismissals.

FAIR PROCEDURES
Lack of fair procedures will automatically lead to a finding of unfair dismissal.

Fair procedures will include, *inter alia*, the necessity to carry out an adequate inquiry. Briefly, fair procedures should include the following:

- the right to be told what the problem is;
- the right to make representations;
- the right to be heard; and
- if a decision is to be made, the right to make a plea in mitigation.

In the case of incapacity due to illness, it is most important that the employee be examined by a doctor or medical advisor, on behalf of the employer. The results of the examination should be disclosed immediately to the employee and possibly the employee should be called to a meeting to discuss the contents of the medical report. Employees should be involved and advised to get their own doctor and perhaps get their own report. Making the decision on the basis of reports, without the involvement of the employee, is also a mistake. The employee should be advised that the employer is contemplating dismissal on the grounds of capacity.

There is no shortage of model and standard procedures. See, for example, those issued by:

(1) The Health and Safety Authority — useful for dealing with bullying and harassment.
(2) The Labour Court.
(3) The Department of Enterprise, Trade and Employment.

RESIGNATION

A contract of employment may be terminated by the resignation of an employee. However, even where an employee has resigned, the EAT may hold that it is a constructive dismissal. As a general rule, if unequivocal words of resignation are used, the employer is entitled to immediately accept the resignation and act accordingly. However, in *Cafferkey v Metrotech Services Ltd* (UD 932/1998), the EAT held that there may be exceptions to this general rule where special circumstances exist relating to the context in which the decision to resign was taken; for example, in the case of an immature employee or a decision taken in the "heat of the moment" or where "idle words are used under emotional stress which the employer knew or ought to have known were not meant to be taken seriously". In such cases, the EAT said there is a duty on employers to take into account the "special circumstances" of an employee. In *Millett v Shinkwin* (DEE4/2004), the Labour Court fully considered the question of whether an employee is legally entitled to withdraw notice of resignation. The Labour Court stated the "general rule" as follows:

"A resignation is a unilateral act which, if expressed in unambiguous and unconditional terms, brings a contract of employment to an end. The contract cannot be reconstructed by a subsequent unilateral withdrawal of the resignation. Where adequate notice is given, the contract is generally terminated in accordance with its terms and since there is no repudiation the acceptance of the resignation by the employer is not required in order to determine the contract."

See also *Martin v Yeoman Aggregates Ltd* ([1983] I.R.L.R. 48) and *Kwik-Fit (GB) Ltd v Linehan* ([1992] I.R.L.R. 156).

REDRESS FOR UNFAIR DISMISSAL

Under the legislation, a claim for redress may be brought by the employee before a Rights Commissioner or the EAT, within the period of six months beginning on the date of the relevant dismissal, or if exceptional circumstances prevented the giving of the notice within the period aforesaid, then, within such period not exceeding 12 months from the date aforesaid as the Rights Commissioner or the EAT considers reasonable (s.8). There is an appeal within six weeks of the recommendation of a Rights Commissioner to the EAT and where the matter went at first instance to the EAT there is an appeal to the Circuit Court (s.9). Where there is a dismissal connected with an employee's pregnancy, a claim may be brought under the Unfair Dismissals Act or under the Employment Equality Act 1998 (see *A Company v A Worker* (DEE6/2001) and *Emmerdale Ltd v A Worker* (DEE5/2002)).

Where an employee is dismissed and the dismissal is held to be an unfair dismissal, the employee shall be entitled to redress consisting of whichever of the following the Rights Commissioner, the EAT or the Circuit Court, as the case may be, considers appropriate, having regard to all the circumstances (s.7(1)):

(a) re-instatement;
(b) re-engagement; and
(c) compensation not exceeding 4 weeks' remuneration where there has been no financial losses incurred, otherwise compensation up to 104 weeks' remuneration.

In assessing compensation, the 1993 Act provides that no account is taken of unemployment benefit or assistance received and no account is taken of income tax rebates. See *Allen v Independent Newspapers (Ireland) Ltd* ([2002] E.L.R. 84), where the factors to be taken into account in awarding compensation were considered.

The EAT has an absolute discretion to choose which remedy to award "having regard to all the circumstances" (see *Keeler v Trademet Ltd* (UD 142/1999) and *Murphy v Neolith Ltd* (UD 337/2001)). However, it is now obliged to set out, where a specified redress is awarded, a statement of the reasons why either of the other forms of redress were not awarded (s.8(1A)). In *Sheehan v Continental Administration Co Ltd* (UD 858/1999), the EAT set out at some length why it considered neither reinstatement nor re-engagement as being the appropriate remedy. The EAT stated that both "these remedies cannot be considered, if, firstly there exists a very definite possibility that it would result in compelling a reluctant employer to continue a relationship of employer/employee, a relationship which is founded on mutual trust and understanding and secondly, the performance of the returning employee may require consistent supervision to ensure adequate performance of duties". Neither will re-instatement or re-engagement be considered where there is the possibility that the award has the potential to create "future friction, disharmony and possibly an acrimonious relationship which could spill over into other areas and cause a disruptive work environment resulting in a decrease in productivity or performance. The more senior the position in the company the greater the care necessitated by the Tribunal in assessing the appropriate remedy." In *State (Irish Pharmaceutical Union) v Employment Appeals Tribunal* ([1987] I.L.R.M. 36), the Supreme Court said that the views of the parties should be sought on the issue of redress before the decision on choice of remedy is taken (see further Chapter 8).

A dismissed employee has the choice of litigating his claim through the civil courts for wrongful dismissal. This can be of benefit where the employee lacks the qualifying service period in order to proceed under the legislation.

SUSPENSION

An employee may be suspended from work either because of misconduct, incompetence or incapacity. Suspension is where an employer absents an employee from work temporarily. Suspension thus stops short of termination. It may, however, be a precursor to a termination. An employee will usually be suspended either as a disciplinary measure or pending an investigation into alleged misconduct, incompetence or incapacity. Suspension may be with or without pay but if the suspension is to be without pay the contract must clearly authorise it. Although there should be a legal basis for a suspension such as an express term in a contract authorising suspension, in certain circumstances the courts may in the absence of such an express contractual term imply such a term into a contract. However, it is only in exceptional circumstances that a court will imply a term suspending without pay (see, for example, *Lawe v Irish Country Meats (Pig Meats) Ltd* ([1998] E.L.R. 266)).

Even where there is a legal basis for a suspension, the exercise of any such power must only occur in circumstances where the employer is acting bona fide in the interests of the employee concerned and/or also in its own interests so as to protect itself from any possible contention that it has failed to properly deal with the interests not only of the employee concerned but also other employees and, potentially, other persons with whom the employer is involved. The period for which an employee is kept out of work on suspension must be kept to a minimum (see *Mary Becker v The Board of Management of St Dominic's Secondary School, Cabra* [2005] 1 I.R. 561). See also *Martin v Nationwide Building Society* ([2001] 1 I.R. 228), where a delay in completing an investigation into wrongdoing during which the plaintiff was suspended was found to be "inordinate and unjust".

Where an employee is wrongfully suspended without pay from work, a claim may lie against the employer for the remuneration he/she would have earned during the period of suspension. A claim may also lie where an employee suffers damage to reputation as a result of a wrongful or unnecessary suspension.

REDUNDANCY

An employee's contract may be terminated by reason of redundancy. The statutes governing redundancy—of which there are five—are collectively cited as the Redundancy Payments Acts 1967–2003. The principal Act came into operation on January 1, 1968 and has been amended by the Protection of Employment Acts 1977–2003. The main thrust of these Acts is to ensure that a redundancy is a genuine one and not a sham redundancy. Even where a redundancy is genuine the Acts require that the selection of an employee for redundancy is not arbitrary and that the employee who is made redundant is appropriately compensated by way of monetary compensation (see s.7). There is a time-limit in which a claim for redundancy payment must be made (see s.24). The period in which to claim may be extended for just cause. On whether the failure to lodge a claim in time was due to a "reasonable cause", see *Clancy v Beau Monde Ltd* (945/1977) and *Comiskey v Beau Monde Ltd* (99/1978). If an employee refuses to accept suitable alternative employment, he/she will not be entitled to redundancy payment (see s.15, 1967 Act).

There is an obligation on an employer to not later than two weeks before the date of dismissal by reason of redundancy give an employee with the requisite service period a notice in writing of the proposed dismissal and send a copy of that notice to the relevant government Minister.

The Acts in no way impinge on the ability of an employer to dismiss for redundancy. All that the Acts require is that if there is a redundancy that it is a genuine one carried out in accordance with the legislation. In *Moon v Homeworthy Furniture Ltd* ([1977] I.C.R. 117), it was held that the function of the EAT is to decide whether there was a redundancy situation and not to decide why the redundancy occurred (see also *Roche v Sealink Stena Line Ltd* (UD 187/1992), reported at ([1993] E.L.R. 89); *Boucher v Irish Productivity Centre* (UD 882/1992), reported at ([1994] E.L.R. 205); and *Hurley v Royal Cork Yacht Club* ([1999] E.L.R. 7)).

Excluded Employees

Excluded from the application of the Acts are employees who do not have the qualifying service period, employments where the employer is the father, mother, grandfather, grandmother, stepfather, stepmother, in *loco parentis,* son, daughter, grandson, granddaughter, stepson, stepdaughter, brother, sister, half-brother or half-sister of the employee, or where the employee is a member of the employer's household and the employment is related to a private dwelling house or a farm in or on which both the employer and the employee reside.

Neither shall the Acts apply to a person who, on the date of termination of his employment, has attained the age which on that date is the pensionable age within the meaning of the Social Welfare (Consolidation) Act 1993 (s.3 of the Redundancy Payments Act 1971 (as amended and adapted)). Other excepted employments are "employment of a casual nature otherwise than for the purposes of the employer's trade or business and otherwise than for the purpose of any game or recreation where the persons are employed through a club, employment specified in regulations as being of such a nature that it is ordinarily adopted as subsidiary employment only and not as the principal means of livelihood and employment specified in regulations as being of inconsiderable extent".

Defining a "Redundancy"

An employee who is dismissed, laid off or kept on short time for a period of four or more consecutive weeks, or for a period of six or more weeks which are not consecutive but which fall within a period of 13 consecutive weeks shall be taken to be dismissed by reason of redundancy if the dismissal is attributed wholly or mainly to:

(a) the fact that his employer has ceased or intends to cease to carry on the business for the purposes of which the employee was employed by him or has ceased or intends to cease to carry on that business in the place where the employee was so employed; or

(b) the fact that the requirements of that business for employees to carry out work of a particular kind in the place where he was so employed have ceased or diminished or are expected to cease or diminish; or

(c) the fact that an employer has decided to carry on the business with fewer or no employees, whether by requiring the work for which the employee has been employed or had been doing before his dismissal, to be done by other employees or otherwise; or

(d) the fact that his employer has decided that the work for which the employee has been employed (or had been doing before the dismissal) should henceforth be done in a different manner for which the employee is not sufficiently qualified or trained; or

(e) the fact that his employer has decided that the work for which the employee has been employed (or had been doing before his dismissal) should henceforth be done by a person who is also capable of doing other work for which the employee is not sufficiently qualified or trained.

See s.7(2) of the 1967 Act, as amended.

Redundancy is defined in each of the five Acts. A common thread in each definition is the characteristics of "impersonality" and "change".

See *St Ledger v Frontline Distributors Ireland Ltd* ([1995] E.L.R. 160), where the EAT said that the statutory definition of "redundancy" has two important characteristics, namely "impersonality" and "change". Redundancy for the purpose of the Acts goes beyond an excess of manpower resulting from mechanisation, rationalisation, or from a decrease in business activity and requiring a permanent reduction in the number of persons employed. The focus is not just on the kind of work but also on the type of employee. The EAT has held that night work is different to day work and that temporary work is different to full time work (see *Dimworth v Southern Health Board* and *Kelleher v St. James's Hospital* (UD 284/77)).

What is "impersonality"?

Impersonality means that the redundancy impacts on the job and only as a consequence of the redundancy does the person involved lose his/her job.

What is "change"?

Change means qualitative change and not quantitative change; it is work of a different kind, a change in the workplace (the most dramatic change of all being a complete close down), a reduction in need for employees, or a reduction in number, a change in the way the work is done or some other form of change in the nature of the job (see *St Ledger*). However, a quantitative change in a downward direction in the volume of work might imply redundancy in circumstances where because of the reduced workload fewer employees may be required.

Ability versus Training?

In *St Ledger,* the EAT also emphasised that training was not the same as ability and said that it was irrelevant that the claimant's replacement was better able to do the work previously done by the claimant. "To hold otherwise", the EAT concluded, "would be to deny the essential impersonality of redundancy". The views of the EAT have been given statutory form by the insertion of the words "for one or more reasons not related to the employee concerned" (see s.5(2) of the Redundancy Payments Act 2003).

Wholly or Mainly

The meaning of the words "attributable wholly or mainly to" in the equivalent British legislation was considered in *Hindle v Percival Boats Ltd* ([1969] 1 W.L.R. 174), where the Court of Appeal held that the onus of proving that dismissal was not attributable to redundancy was discharged if the employer satisfied the Tribunal that the reason he gave was genuine and was the main reason for the dismissal, even though that reason was based on a mistaken view of the facts. Thus, a two-step cumulative test applies; the reason for the redundancy must be genuine and it must be the main reason.

Diminution in work

A diminution in the work means a diminution in the requirement for employees to do that work (*McCrea v Cullen & Dawson Ltd* ([1988] I.R.L.R. 30). See also *Keenan v Gresham Hotel Co. Ltd* (UD478/1988)).

Place of Work

In *Bass Leisure Ltd v Thomas* ([1994] I.R.L.R. 104), the English EAT said that the place of employment should be established "by a factual inquiry, taking into account the employee's fixed or changing place or places of work and any contractual terms which go to evidence or define the place of employment." In this case, the fact that the contract provided that the company reserved the right to transfer any employee to a suitable alternative place of work did not result in the claimant losing her right to a redundancy payment when she resigned after being relocated to a depot some 20 miles away. This was upheld on appeal. In *Broderick v Dorothea Fashions Ltd* (RP 11/1978), the EAT held that East Arran Street was not the same place as Churchtown and in *Earley v Floorstyle Contracts Ltd* (RP382/2003), it was held that Skerries was not the same place as Swords.

Continuous Employment

The meaning of the words "continuous employment" was considered in *Irish Shipping Ltd v Adams* ((1987) 6 J.I.S.L.L. 186). The claimants were all seamen who served varying periods of engagement on different ships with varying periods elapsing between engagements. The EAT took the view that the periods of elapsement were merely lay-offs and did not affect continuity of service. The Act provides, *inter alia*, where an employee's period of service is interrupted by a period of not more than 26 consecutive weeks by reason of holidays, lay-offs or any cause—other than the voluntary leaving of his/her employment, authorised by the employer—continuity of employment shall not be broken. On appeal to the High Court, it was held that the EAT was entitled as a matter of law to come to the decision it did and the appeal was dismissed. See also *Daly v Wessel Cable Ltd* (UD 651/1986) and *Hayes v O'Kelly Bros Civil Engineering Ltd* (UD268/2001).

Collective Redundancies

A collective redundancy occurs where there are a number of employees made redundant. Collective redundancies require specific procedures. There is both a notification and a consultation obligation on the employer (see s.9). Consultation should be done with the possibility of avoiding the proposed redundancies, reducing the number of employees affected by them or mitigating their consequences by recourse to accompanying social measures such as, *inter alia*, redeploying or retraining employees. Employees to be made redundant should be informed of the basis on which selection will be decided and which particular employees will be made redundant. Consultations must be initiated at the earliest opportunity and in any event at least 30 days before the first dismissal takes effect. The question of precisely when an employer can be said to be proposing to create collective redundancies was considered by the English EAT in *Hough v Leyland DAF Ltd* ([1991] I.R.L.R. 194), where it was held that this occurred when matters had reached a stage where a specific proposal had been formulated, which was at a later stage than the diagnosis of a problem and the appreciation that at least one way of dealing with it would be by declaring redundancies. In *R. v British Coal Corporation, ex parte Vardy* ([1993] I.R.L.R. 104), it was held that the relevant EU Directive required that consultation begin as soon as an employer contemplates redundancies. However, in *Griffin v South West Water Services Ltd* ([1995] I.R.L.R. 15), it was felt that the obligation to consult only arose when the employer's contemplation of redundancies had reached the point where it was able to identify the workers likely to be affected and could supply the required information. It was not open to an employer to argue that consultation would be futile or utterly useless.

Relevant information relating to the proposed redundancies which must be supplied in writing includes (see s.10):

> (a) the reasons for the proposed redundancies;

(b) the number, and descriptions or categories, of employees whom it is proposed to make redundant;

(c) the number of employees, and description of categories, normally employed; and

(d) the period during which it is proposed to effect the proposed redundancies;

(e) the criteria proposed for the selection of the workers to be made redundant; and

(f) the method of calculating any redundancy payments other than those methods set out in the Redundancy Payments Acts 1967–2003 or any other relevant enactment for the time being in force or, subject thereto, in practice.

Essentially, there should be sufficient information to enable the employees' respresentatives to make constructive proposals (see *General and Municipal Workers Union v British Uralite Ltd* ([1979] I.R.L.R. 409, 412)).

An employer must, as soon as possible, supply the relevant Minister with copies of all information supplied in writing.

Selection Process

Criteria used when selecting employees for redundancy should be capable of objective verification. For example, selection made at the discretion of the Managing Director is not capable of objective verification and would not be a wise choice, whereas selection made on the basis of criteria which are directly referable to records, such as disciplinary and time records and criteria relating to the possession of certain qualifications and those relating to employees who have undergone certain training, would be a better choice. Selection criteria that might constitute indirect discrimination would also be questionable and should be avoided. In *Williams v Compare Maxon Ltd* ([1982] I.R.L.R. 83), the English Court of Appeal set out the following check list for employers faced with selecting employees for redundancy.

1. There must be a warning advising in advance or as soon as possible that redundancies are contemplated.

2. The employer should consult with the Unions in relation to, if possible, agreeing selection criteria. Further consultation should take place in relation to whether the employees selected meet those criteria.

3. Whether or not criteria have been agreed, the criteria used for the selection should be capable of being objectively verified and as far as possible should not be dependent solely on the opinion of the person making the selection.
4. The employees to be made redundant should be selected for redundancy only on the basis of those criteria and the employer should hear any representations by the Union in relation to the selections made.
5. The employer should consider the possibility of alternative employment in the company.
6. If the principle of LIFO (last in first out) is being used, the employer should be careful that it is properly applied. For example, where length of service is the criteria, the employer should be careful to calculate the service of the employees correctly.

In *McMillan v Comerof Ltd* (1997 I.L.R. 85), the employer only calculated a particular portion of service in a particular line of work and this was held to be an unfair selection because the entire service should be counted and, if so, the complainant employee would not have been let go.

In light of the Part-Time and Fixed-Term Work Acts, a person's status as a part-time or fixed-term worker should not be used as the basis for selection.

Redress

Disputes may be referred to Deciding Officers. If a party is unhappy with a decision of a Deciding Officer the matter may be referred to the EAT. Any dispute arising under a special redundancy scheme may be referred by a party to the scheme to the EAT (see s.15(1) of the Redundancy Payments Act 1971). Where a dispute concerns whether there was in fact a redundancy or whether it was a dismissal disguised as a redundancy, the matter may be referred to the EAT, with an appeal lying to the Circuit Court and thereafter to the High Court on a point of law. If it is found that there was a dismissal rather than a redundancy, redress may lie for unfair dismissal.

8. REDRESS, REMEDIES AND ENFORCEMENT

Redress or remedies for breaches of employment law may be pursued at law or in equity (under the law of contract) and/or under the legislation. However, in almost all cases, an election must be made as to whether to pursue a claim through the civil courts or through the statutory tribunals. As to whether an election has been made, see the leading authority of *Parson v Iarnrod Eireann* ([1977] E.L.R. 203). In this case, the plaintiff who was dismissed instituted proceedings under the Unfair Dismissals legislation. The matter went before the Rights Commissioner who gave a recommendation that the plaintiff should proceed to the next stage of the defendant's internal disciplinary proceedings. The plaintiff submitted to the next stage where his dismissal was affirmed and following which the plaintiff instituted proceedings in the High Court seeking damages for wrongful dismissal. The defendant applied to have the proceedings struck out as the plaintiff had taken steps in a statutory action. The High Court struck out the proceedings and said that the plaintiff must indeed choose and had in fact chosen the statutory remedy.

Though it is said that redress and remedies differ depending on whether an employee pursues an action at law or under the legislation, their effect can be the same. The remedy in the civil courts will generally be damages or the equitable remedies of specific performance, declaratory relief and/or injunctive relief. Statutory redress may be compensation (which is similar to damages), re-instatement or re-engagement (which can have the same effect as specific performance/injunctive relief). Redress may require an employer to comply with the provisions of the legislation, such as the granting of maternity, parental, adoptive or carer's leave with or without compensation or a requirement to pay the minimum wage with or without compensation. Where an action is taken under the legislation, the maximum amount of compensation awarded and the method for calculating same will be laid down in the various statutes, but where an action is taken through the civil courts, the maximum amount of damages will depend on the jurisdictional limits of the court.

Redress	Remedies
Under the Legislation	**Through the Civil Courts**
Compensation	Damages
Re-instatement	Injunction/Specific Performance
Re-engagement	Injunction Declaration

In appropriate cases, judicial review with its remedies of *certiorari* or *mandamus* may be available.

MAKING THE ELECTION

A claimant may be faced with a multiplicity of remedies. In this situation, the claimant must make an election as to which to pursue; either maintain an action in the civil courts or maintain a statutory cause of action under the legislation in the statutory tribunals. Making the election will involve an assessment of factors such as: the adequacy of each remedy, *viz.* what redress it will yield; will there be a cost jeopardy (the cost of pursuing that remedy as against the value of any likely redress); is there a temporal jeopardy — the time it will take to bring the remedy home may be crucial; the likelihood of success; and which action is likely to give the aggrieved party the outcome he/she desires. However, there is no reason why actions may not be instituted initially through both the statutory tribunals and the court and the election made at a later stage in the process but before any step is taken in a hearing in either. A step is taken where the hearing by a Tribunal or court has commenced.

Sometimes only one remedy will be available to an employee, *viz.* an employee in question lacks the requisite service period to avail of the protection of the legislation or is an excluded employee. Thus, in an action for dismissal, an employee who lacks the requisite service period may take a common law action for wrongful dismissal where the only time constraint is that the action be brought within the limitation period set down by the Statute of Limitations 1957, *viz.* six years for actions in contract.

As stated above, factors which will influence/affect the election are:

- Is there a cost jeopardy or only a minimal one?
- What remedies does each forum yield?
- The length of time taken to yield the remedy.

TYPES OF REMEDIES/REDRESS

Redress Under the Legislation

As already stated, redress under the legislation for the most part will be compensation, re-instatement, re-engagement or a combination of compensation and re-instatement or re-engagement, and in appropriate cases, the employer will be required to comply with his/her obligations under the statutory provisions. Compensation is usually the preferred option, re-instatement and re-engagement only being offered where the relationship of trust and confidence still remains between the employer and employee.

Redress under the legislation is pursued through one of the Statutory Tribunals and the particular statute will dictate which and also the procedural requirements and time limits.

Re-instatement

Re-instatement has the effect of undoing the dismissal by re-instating the dismissed employee back into the position held immediately prior to the dismissal (see s.7(1)(a), Unfair Dismissals Act 1977 and see *Hurley v Royal Cork Yacht Club* ([1999] E.L.R. 7) where "re-instatement was deemed to have taken place on the date of dismissal"). If, during the period of the dismissal the terms and conditions of the other members of a group to which the dismissed employee belonged were improved by way of salary increase or otherwise, the reinstated employee must be given these improved terms and conditions. In other words, the dismissal should not have had any effect whatsoever. Importantly, the dismissal would not break continuity of service of the employee in question.

As stated above, re-instatement will not usually be ordered where the relationship of trust and confidence has broken down between the parties. This is the approach of both the statutory tribunals and the Courts to re-instatement. See *Moore v Xnet Information Systems* ([2002] 2 I.L.R.M. 278), where the High Court held that re-instatement pending the hearing of the case would not be granted because relations "between the plaintiff and defendant have irretrievably broken down". In *Bergin v Dublin Bus,* re-instatement was ordered where the employee had been dismissed for misconduct in circumstances where he should not have been so dismissed. Re-instatement may be granted more readily in cases where it is re-instatement to a prior position rather than back into the current position (see *Revenue Commissioners v Cantillon* (EE6/ 1985 DEE 7/1985). Re-instatement may also be an appropriate remedy in cases where an employee has been suspended. In *Connolly v McConnell* ([1983] I.R. 172), the defendant sought a declaration in the High Court that he was still in office as financial general secretary of the plaintiff Union and also sought damages for wrongful dismissal. Because of the failure by the plaintiff Union to comply with the requirements of natural justice and failure to adopt correct procedures, the purported dismissal of the defendant was held to be void. Reinstatement was ordered.

An order directing the re-instatement (or re-engagement) of the employee concerned may be amended by the Circuit Court, where it considers it appropriate to do so having regard to all the circumstances (s.11, 1993 Act). In these circumstances, the Circuit Court makes an order directing the employer, in lieu of re-instating or re-engaging the employee, to pay compensation.

Re-engagement

Re-engagement is essentially a lesser form of re-instatement. Whereas re-instatement requires that the worker goes back into the same job, re-engagement only requires that the worker be re-employed either in the same job or in an appropriate or suitable different job. The Act of 1977 defines re-engagement as being either a return to the position which was held immediately before the dismissal or to a different position which would be reasonably suitable and on such terms and conditions as are reasonable, having regard to all the circumstances (s.7(1)(b)). As with re-instatement, re-engagement will not be ordered where the relationship between employer and employee has deteriorated badly or where, because of changes, no suitable job is available. See, for example, *Stewart v Unifi Textured Yarns* ([1999] E.L.R. 276), where the EAT said that in view "of the issues of contention between the parties re-employment in any form was not an appropriate remedy". Where re-engagement is ordered, either by the Statutory Tribunal or by the courts, it is done on whatever terms the Tribunal or court deems fit. This is quite a wide discretion and is generally exercised in the following way: if there has been, say, 18 months since a dismissal, re-engagement might be ordered back-dated for, say, 12 months and the other six months deemed leave without pay.

Compensation

Compensation is a monetary award. It is the preferred remedy where re-instatement or re-engagement are, for whatever reason, unsuitable. See, for example, *McMahon v Securicor Omega Express Limited* ([2002] E.L.R. 317) where compensation was considered appropriate as the claimant had found other work. Compensation is on a "just and equitable" basis up to a maximum amount, as defined in the particular statute under which the action is taken. The maximum is usually referable to the employee's remuneration and remuneration includes benefits in kind, in addition to wages or salary. The financial losses, actual and estimated, incurred by the employee can sometimes be relevant in calculating compensation but there is a duty on the employee to mitigate his/her losses. See *Marie Inoue v NBK Designs* ([2003] E.L.R. 98), where €10,000 was awarded for discrimination and where the claimant's actual loss was €1,400 (see also *Cox v Healy t/a Convenience Express* ([1992] E.L.R. 125)).

Redress through the Civil Courts

When the action is taken through the civil courts, it will generally be an action for breach of contract and all of the normal contractual remedies such as damages, rectification and rescission will apply. The equitable remedies of specific performance and injunction will also be available. In appropriate cases, judicial review may be pursued as seen below.

Damages

The amount of damages awarded in an action through the civil courts will depend on the jurisdictional limits of the court in which the action is taken and will be limited to those losses which foreseeably flow from the breach. The basis of assessment will be actual loss and potential loss of earnings, general damages including compensation for loss of job and, where appropriate, compensation for the manner and circumstances in which the dismissal was carried out. Where the employee has contributed to the grievance, there may be a reduction in the amount of the award (see *Carney v Balkan Tours Ltd* ([1997] E.L.R. 102)).

Specific Performance

Specific performance is an equitable remedy and like all equitable remedies is a discretionary remedy. As a general rule, contracts for personal services will not be specifically enforced. See, for example, *Lift Manufacturers Ltd v Irish Life Assurance Co. Ltd* ([1979] I.L.R.M. 227), where the court said that the principle that specific performance will not be granted in respect of a contract for services is not a rigid one and where there appears to be no reason or necessity for the court to supervise performance of the contract, an argument against enforcement by way of specific performance cannot apply. See also *C.H. Giles & Co. v Morris* ([1972] 1 W.L.R. 307) and *Hill v Parsons & Co. Ltd* ([1972] Ch. 305). The employment contract is such a contract for personal services. Thus, this remedy is of limited value in an employment context.

Injunction

The equitable remedy of injunction was developed to provide relief where the traditional common law remedy of damages was either inadequate or inappropriate. Traditionally, injunctions were used in the employment area to restrain trade only, and were granted in favour of the employer in cases where the contract between the employer and employee contained a clause in restraint of trade. The injunction as a remedy was traditionally restricted to these type of cases because the courts felt that the remedies of injunction, like specific performance, were unsuitable remedies for contracts of employment. This was because the result of these remedies was to force two parties to continue in a relationship which had a personal element and which at least one party had no desire to continue and rather than force the relationship to continue the courts felt the better approach was to regulate the split.

Whereas the courts lean against granting injunctions in employment law cases, there are many cases where an interim/interlocutory injunction has been granted to maintain the *status quo* pending the hearing of an action but they will only be granted in circumstances where a common law action has been instituted and subject to the *Campus Oil v Minister for Industry (No.2)* principles (see *Parsons v Iarnrod Éireann* and *Johnson v Unisys Limited* ([2003] 1 A.C. 518)).

Before deciding whether to grant interloctury injunctive relief, the guiding principles are set out in *Campus Oil v Minister for Industry (No.2)* ([1983] I.R. 82). These guiding principles are:

- there must be a fair issue to be tried;
- damages would not be an adequate remedy; and
- the balance of convenience must lie in favour of granting the injunction.

These guiding principles were reiterated by the court in *Orr v Zomas Ltd* ([2004] I.R. 486), where the plaintiff sought injunctive relief restraining the termination of his employment and directing the payment of his salary pending the trial of the action. In deciding whether or not to grant injunctive relief directing that an employer pay salary pending the trial of the action, the courts tend to take into account the financial circumstances of the plaintiff and the fact that a plaintiff would be left without a salary and have nothing to live on (see *Hill v Parsons & Co* ([1972] Ch. 305) and *Fennelly v Assicurazioni Generali Soa* (1985) 3 I.L.T.R. 73). A plaintiff does not necessarily have to establish penury to obtain relief (see *Harte v Kelly* ([1997] E.L.R. 125)).

Other factors that may influence a court in deciding whether or not to grant this type of injunction include the estimated length of time to the hearing of the main action and whether trust and confidence between the parties still exists.

Regarding the issue of whether there is a fair question to be tried, see *Mary Becker v The Board of Management of St Dominic's Secondary School, Cabra* ([2005] 1 I.R. 561), where the High Court held that the question as to whether there was any legal basis for the plaintiff's suspension and whether the defendant was acting mala fide in suspending the plaintiff was a fair question to be tried. In *Fennelly v Assicurazioni Generali Soa,* the matter as to whether the plaintiff's contract had been invalidly terminated was held to be a fair question to be tried.

If damages are an adequate remedy, an injunction will not be granted. The remedy of damages will generally be considered to be adequate if the plaintiff does not wish or "cannot seriously hope that he will be re-instated in employment where the defendant is unwilling to take him back and has no place for him. Therefore, his remedy, if successful, is in damages" (see, for example, *Orr v Zomas Ltd* ([2004] I.R. 486, 494)).

On where the balance of convenience lies, see, for example, *Mary Becker v The Board of Management of St Dominic's Secondary School, Cabra,* where the High Court held that the "balance of convenience favoured refusing the injunction, in particular as a forced absence from work for a short period pending a medical examination would not impose an excessive burden on a plaintiff who had been absent from work for 160 days in the previous short number of years". In *Michael Foley v Aer Lingus Group plc* ([2001] E.L.R. 193), where the claimant sought an interlocutory injunction restraining the defendant from appointing another person in his place pending the hearing of his action for unfair dismissal and damage to reputation, the High Court in refusing the injunction held that the balance of convenience favoured the defendant due to the hardship and difficulty the company would face without the services of a CEO to replace the plaintiff.

Judicial Review

Judicial review may be available to an aggrieved employee either because he/she is in the employment of the State or a State sponsored company or because the statutory tribunals are bodies subject to judicial review. Judicial review is an application to the High Court to either have a decision or order of a lower court or tribunal quashed or to obtain an order directing a lower court or tribunal to take a certain action (Ord.84 of the Rules of the Superior Courts). It is immaterial whether the decision sought to be quashed was correct or not on the merits. Orders available by way of judicial review that may be relevant in employment are orders of *certiorari* (an order to quash a decision) and *mandamus* (an order directing a lower court or tribunal to fulfil or carry out a lawful obligation which it has not fulfilled or carried out).

An applicant for judicial review must firstly seek the leave of the High Court and this leave will not generally issue where there is an alternative remedy by way of appeal to another body, *e.g.* where there is a right of appeal to the Circuit Court from a decision of the EAT (see for example, *Mooney v An Post* ([1998] 4 I.R. 288) and see *Maher v Irish Permanent Plc* ([1998] 4 I.R. 302)).

Before an applicant will be granted leave to apply for judicial review he/she must satisfy the following test:

- The applicant must demonstrate that he/she has sufficient interest in the matter to which the application refers.
- That the facts, if proved, to support a stateable ground for the form of relief sought by way of judicial review.
- That on those facts an arguable case in law can be made that the applicant is entitled to the relief which he/she seeks.

- That the application has been made promptly and in any event within the permitted time limits of three or six months unless the applicant can satisfy the court that there is good reason for extending these time limits.
- That the only effective remedy which the applicant could obtain would be an order by way of judicial review or if there is an alternative remedy the application by way of judicial review is the more appropriate method to achieve a remedy.

See *G v DPP* ([1994] 1 I.R. 374).

Judicial review is concerned with whether the lower court, tribunal or administrative body acted *intra vires* (within its powers), or *ultra vires* (outside its powers), and where it did act *intra vires,* did it comply with procedures including compliance with the basic rules of natural and constitutional justice and fair procedures, *viz. nemo judex in causa sua* and *audi alteram partem.* See, for example, *Mooney v An Post* [1998] 4 I.R. 288 and *Maher v Irish Permanent plc* [1998] 4 I.R. 302.

Judicial review in the area of employment can be traced back to the judgment of Walsh J. in *Glover v BLN Ltd* [1973] I.R. 388, where the plaintiff was awarded damages arising out of his dismissal as company director because the decision to dismiss was taken without allowing the plaintiff a hearing. On appeal to the Supreme Court, it was held that it was immaterial whether the plaintiff was an office holder to whom a right to a hearing had traditionally been afforded or was merely an employee employed under contract, since "public policy and the dictates of constitutional justice require that statutes, regulations or agreements setting up machinery for taking decisions which may affect rights or impose liabilities should be construed as providing for fair procedures" (see also *Gunn v Bord an Choláiste Náisiúnta Ealaine is Deartha* ([1990] 2 I.R. 193). In *Daly v Department of Agriculture,* judicial review was used where there was a failure by the State Employer to make an appointment.

Judicial review was successfully used in *State (Ferris) v Employment Appeals Tribunal* ([1985] 4 J.I.S.S.L. 100), a case which concerned a refusal by the EAT to accept jurisdiction in a claim for damages for unfair dismissal. Because the EAT had wrongly concluded that an election had been made to take proceedings in the civil courts, the applicant/employee was granted an order of *certiorari* quashing the decision of the EAT refusing jurisdiction.

In *Mythen v EAT*, *certiorari* was granted to quash a determination of the EAT. It was held that the EAT had made an error of law which goes to jurisdiction and the appropriate remedy was an order of *certiorari* and that the applicant should not be denied the relief of such an order just because he could instead have appealed to the Circuit Court.

In *Caldwell & Others v The Labour Court* ([1988] 2 I.R. 280), a case which involved a claim for equal pay for equal work under the relevant legislation, the claimants, female employees, took their case to the ODEI, whose Equality Officer made a recommendation in their favour. The recommendation was successfully appealed to the Labour Court by the employer. The claimants applied in the High Court for relief by way of judicial review seeking an order of *certiorari* quashing the order of the Labour Court, on the basis that the Labour Court had acted *ultra vires*.

Judicial review can avail both employer and employee alike. See *Nova Colour Graphic Supplies Limited v EAT & Brian Spain* ([1987] 3 I.R. 426), where the applicant employer obtained an order of *certiorari* quashing an award of EAT, on the basis that the EAT lacked jurisdiction to make the award.

The High Court has jurisdiction in judicial review applications to grant other remedies in addition to *certiorari* and *mandamus,* such as an award of damages or declaratory relief.

Notwithstanding that judicial review has been successfully availed of in employment cases, the Supreme Court has indicated a preference for the utilising of statutory tribunals for the resolving of employment disputes. See the *obiter dictum* in *Mary Fuller & Others v Minister for Agriculture and Food and the Minister for Finance* ([2005] I.R. 529), wherein the Supreme Court said that the Oireachtas has through legislation 'provided a framework for the resolution of industrial disputes and had established bodies such as the Labour Relations Commission, the Labour Court and other specialists negotiation and arbitration bodies to this end." See also *Patrick O'Donnell v Tipperary (South Riding) County Council* ([2005] I.R. 483) where the Supreme Court said that "in the context of common sense and the ability to deal with questions raised ... an appeal to the Employment Appeals Tribunal was the more appropriate remedy".

VENUES FOR REDRESS

Venue in which to seek redress are the statutory tribunals and the civil courts. The statutory tribunals are:

- The Labour Relations Commission.
- The Labour Court.
- The Employment Appeals Tribunal.
- The Equality Tribunal.

There is also a body known as the Equality Authority but this is not a venue in which to litigate a claim.

The Labour Relations Commission

The Labour Relations Commission (LRC) was established under the Industrial Relations Act. The Commission is composed of a Chairperson and six Ordinary Members, two of whom are trade union nominees, two employer representatives and two people nominated directly by the Minister. On request, the LRC appoints an Industrial Relations Officer who facilitates meetings between the parties in dispute and attempts to find an acceptable resolution.

The LRC comprises three sections and provides the following services:

- A Conciliation Service that assists employers and unions to resolve industrial relations disputes.
- An Advisory Development and Research Service that works with employers and unions to build and maintain good industrial and employment relations. In addition, it undertakes research, monitors industrial relations developments and helps to prepare Codes of Practice.
- The Rights Commissioner Service which performs a role under various employment legislation as well as assisting in disputes involving an individual or small groups of employees. A Rights Commissioner assigned by the LRC will meet with the parties and later issue a recommendation on the issue in dispute. Recommendations from a Rights Commissioner may be appealed either to the EAT or to the Labour Court, and on a point of law to the High Court.

The Labour Court

The Labour Court was established under the 1946 Industrial Relations Act. The role of the Labour Court has been modified over the years by the various Industrial Relations Acts. The court consists of a Chairperson, two Deputy Chairpersons and six Ordinary Members. The court operates on the basis of three separate divisions, each comprised of the Chairperson or a Deputy Chairperson and two Ordinary Members. Half of the Ordinary Members are nominees of the ICTU and the other half from employer organisations.

In industrial relations matters, the court's role is to give a considered opinion in the form of a recommendation as to the terms in which a particular dispute should be settled. The parties to a dispute can either accept or reject this opinion. When dealing with appeals made under the equality legislation and under the provisions of the Industrial Relations (Amendment) Act 2001, the court can make determinations which have a legal standing.

Disputes must normally be referred first to the Labour Relations Commission for conciliation before referral to the court. The Labour Court generally may not investigate unless the Labour Relations Commission is satisfied that conciliation between the parties has failed. There are some exceptions as follows:

- Where the Commission has waived its right to conciliate with the agreement of the parties.
- Where the issue is on appeal from a recommendation of a Rights Commissioner.
- The dispute is referred to the court by the Minister.
- Referrals have been made under s.20 of the Industrial Relations Act 1969.
- Where it is an appeal from a recommendation of an Equality Officer under the employment equality legislation.

The procedures adopted by the court involve a formal presentation of submissions by both parties, followed by questions from the members of the court in respect of the presentations. The court will then issue a recommendation which, in the case of normal industrial relation disputes, is not binding on the parties. However, in the vast majority of cases, recommendations of the court are accepted.

The Employment Appeals Tribunal

The Employment Appeals Tribunal (EAT), referred to as the Tribunal, was set up under s.39 of the Redundancy Payments Act 1967. It was originally known as the Redundancy Appeals Tribunal. Its name was changed by s.18 of the Unfair Dismissals Act 1977. The Tribunal, which is an independent body, consists of a Chairperson and a panel of Vice-Chairpersons with legal qualifications (appointed directly by the Minister) and a panel of other members, nominated by the Irish Congress of Trade Unions and by employer organisations.

The Tribunal ordinarily acts by division, each division consisting of a Chairperson or Vice-Chairperson and two members, each drawn for the respective sides of the panel. The Tribunal is a quasi-judicial court interpreting the terms of the relevant legislation. Appeals of its decisions may be made to the ordinary courts.

The Tribunal deals at first instance with disputes arising under the following Acts:

* Redundancy Payments Acts 1967–2003.
* Minimum Notice and Terms of Employment Acts 1973–2001.
* Unfair Dismissals Acts 1977–2001.
* Protection of Employees (Employers' Insolvency) Act 1984.

The Tribunal has an appellate jurisdiction under the following Acts:

* Terms of Employment (Information) Act 1994.
* Adoptive Leave Acts 1995–2005.
* The Parental Leave Acts 1998–2005.
* Carer's Leave Act 2001.
* Protection of Young Persons (Employment) Act 1996.

Equality Authority

The Employment Equality Agency, established by s.34 of the Employment Equality Act 1977, is now known as the Equality Authority (s.38 of the EEA 1998). The Authority consists of four distinct but integrated sections:

* Legal
* Communications
* Development
* Administration

PROCEDURES INVOLVING LRC AND LABOUR COURT

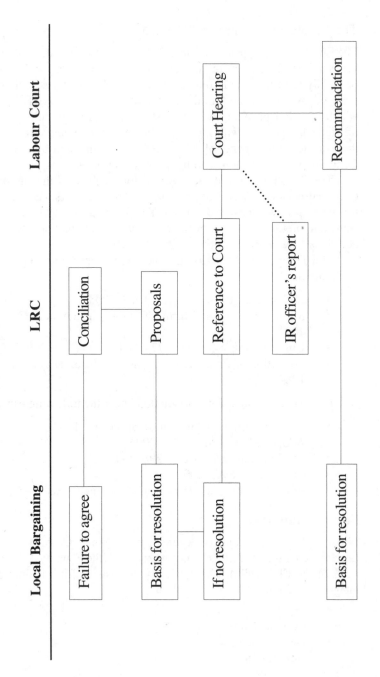

The Equality Authority was set up initially by s.34 of the Employment Equality Act 1977 and by virtue of s.38 of the EEA 1998, which is now known as the Equality Authority. It is not a venue in which to litigate a claim. Its functions are to promote equality, to engage in research, to review the legislation and policy making, and to take suitable cases and institute proceedings on behalf of persons at their discretion. It is certainly possible for an employee of limited resources to apply to the Equality Authority to have their case funded.

The functions of the Authority are:

- to work towards the elimination of discrimination in relation to employment;
- to promote equality of opportunity in relation to the matters to which the Employment Equality Act 1998 applies;
- to provide information to the public on the working of the Parental Leave Act 1998;
- to provide information to the public on and to keep under review, the working of this Act, the Maternity Protection Act 1994, and the Adoptive Leave Act 1995, and, whenever it thinks necessary, to make proposals to the Minister for amending any of those Acts; and
- to keep under review the working of the Pensions Act 1990, as regards the principle of equal treatment and, whenever it thinks necessary, to make proposals to the appropriate government Minister for amending that Act;
- to work towards the elimination of prohibited conduct;
- to promote equality of opportunity in relation to matters to which the Equal Status Act 2000 applies; and
- to provide information to the public on, and to keep under review the working of the 2000 Act and, whenever the Authority thinks it necessary, to make proposals to the Minister for its amendment under the Employment Equality Act 1998.

The Authority has power to refer cases to the Director of Equality Investigations. The Authority may institute summary proceedings in respect of an offence under the Act.

Equality Tribunal

The Equality Tribunal is an entirely different body from the Equality Authority. It was set up under the Employment Equality Act 1998. The Equality Tribunal is an impartial, independent body set up to consider and decide cases brought under the equality laws. Its decisions are legally binding, and it has extensive powers. The Tribunal is a quasi-judicial body. It does not have to decide cases using court procedures, and can follow relatively accessible and informal procedures. It is, however, bound by the principles of natural justice, which means that it considers complaints before it impartially, and ensures fairness for both parties in its procedures. The Tribunal seeks to provide a service which is accessible to both parties. The service is free, and parties are not required to have legal or other representation. The Equality Tribunal is headed by a Director of Equality Investigations and has staff known as Equality Officers and Equality Mediation Officers. Equality Officers investigate and decide cases, and Equality Mediation Officers provide the mediation service. These Officers are civil servants with experience of complex legislation.

The functions of the Equality Tribunal include providing advice and legal representation to those wishing to make a complaint and hearing and deciding cases brought under the employment equality Acts. The Equality Tribunal decides or mediates cases brought under the Employment Equality Act 1998, the Equal Status Act 2000 and Pt VII of the Pensions Acts 1990 as amended by s.22 of the Social Welfare (Miscellaneous Provisions) Act 2004. Under the Employment Equality Act 1998, the Equality Tribunal deals with complaints of discrimination or related conduct based on gender, marital status, family status, age, disability, race (including nationality, colour or ethnic/national origin), religion or belief, sexual orientation or membership of the Traveller community. Generally speaking, the complaints may relate to any aspect of employment, job advertising, or vocational training, including equal pay cases, complaints of direct or indirect discrimination, harassment, sexual harassment, or failure to provide reasonable accommodation for a person with a disability. There are only two exceptions to the general principle that all complaints under the Employment Equality Act 1998 go to the Equality Tribunal and they are: complaints of discriminatory dismissal must be referred to the EAT or referred directly to the Labour Court; and a complainant on the gender ground may choose to refer their complaint to the Circuit Court instead of to the

Labour Court (discriminatory dismissals) or the Equality Tribunal (any other claim).

The Civil Courts

The Circuit Court has original jurisdiction under the Employment Equality Act 1998 in the case of a gender-based discrimination. It has unlimited jurisdiction in this instance. There is an appeal to the High Court which is a full rehearing.

The civil courts also have common law and equitable jurisdiction in employment matters.

The Circuit Court has an appellate jurisdiction in the matter of statutory appeals from the EAT. The appeal in such cases is a full rehearing of the matter. Where a matter under the equality legislation is heard at first instance in the Labour Court, an appeal lies to the Circuit Court.

Common law actions which can be heard in the civil courts include actions for breach of contract for wrongful dismissal, straightforward claims for outstanding remuneration, or bonus or commission.

Index